What
Makes
Israel
Tick

IRA SHARKANSKY

What
Makes
Israel
Tick

How Domestic
Policy-Makers
Cope with
Constraints

Nelson-Hall

nh Chicago

LIBRARY OF CONGRESS CATALOGING IN PUBLICATION DATA

Sharkansky, Ira.
    What makes Israel tick.
    Bibliography: p.
    Includes index.
    1. Israel—Politics and government.   2. Israel—
Economic policy.   I. Title.
DS126.5.S444 1985   956.94'054   84-14854
ISBN 0-8304-1106-2

Manufactured in the United States of America

10   9   8   7   6   5   4   3   2   1

The paper in this book is pH neutral (acid-free)

For Varda

CONTENTS

CONTENTS

PREFACE

When I moved to Israel in 1975, I was attracted to the country as much by intellectual excitement as by a sense of adventure and feelings of emotional involvement. I carried with me more than ten years' experience studying politics and policy making, mostly from the perspectives of universities in Wisconsin and the South. The view that the routines of politics resist change was prominent in my intellectual baggage.[1] While I saw Israel as a new and developing country, I was prepared to find that it, too, is affected by elements beyond the control of its government. As a small country, Israel might be more movable by key officials than the huge and unwieldy United States. However, a small country is more vulnerable to influences outside its borders.

Veteran Israelis are accustomed to asking newcomers what features of the society they would like to change. This question may be put more often than usual to newly arrived professors of public administration. My stock answer was,

"Nothing." Reformers are usually frustrated in their efforts. I had much to learn about the country and its language. I thought of myself as having come to observe the government, rather than to change it—at least in the short run or in major dimensions.

In the course of learning what makes Israel tick, I experienced the frustrations and anxieties, as well as the rewards, of the society. For the first time in my adult life, I screamed in public. My targets were insensitive bureaucrats, who refused to provide anything close to reasonable service. During my first month in the country, a terrorist's bomb went off while I was shopping in the center of Jerusalem. I was intellectually prepared for such an event, but my emotional reactions were strong. On yet another occasion, a bomb exploded within earshot of my seminar at the university. The student who was delivering a paper at the time did not drop a syllable: he continued talking about the differences between the kibbutzim (collective agricultural settlements) that he had studied. When he finished the rest of us asked a few polite questions and then rushed outside. There had been one death and a serious injury. In 1982 I felt excitement, awe, and simple fear as I went north in my military uniform toward an active front.

This book mirrors my observations about policy-making in Israel. Some of the material reflects systematic research. I chose topics that reveal fascinating peculiarities of Israeli politics. Examples are the struggles of Menachem Begin and his party colleagues to learn the craft of government (chapter 3); Israel's religious parties (chapter 4); the changes that occur in budgeting under very high inflation (chapter 5); and Teddy Kollek's Jerusalem Foundation (chapter 6). Some material derives from my participation in the policy-making forums of Hebrew University and the government. Other material comes from countless conversations and much exposure to the mass media.

The result is a book that examines selected topics that should provide insights into the dominant practices that shape Israel's government and through it, the economy and society. To the extent that the analyses succeed in this objective, they will compensate the reader for my failure to cover *every* facet of policy-making.

While the basic nature of Israeli politics may remain in place, the particulars can change. In October 1983, Menachem Begin resigned as prime minister and was replaced by Yitzhak Shamir. The first significant act of the new government was to declare major changes in economic policy. It was Likud's (the dominant political bloc, led by Menachem Begin and then by Yitzhak Shamir) second new economic policy, which, to a large extent, undid the work of the first, promulgated in 1977. With a large devaluation of the shekel (Israel's currency) and sizable cuts in subsidies, the government moved toward renewed control of the economy in the style of the Labour party, which had ruled Israel from 1948 to 1977. Modern Israelis, like those who wrote the Book of Ecclesiastes, were demonstrating that there is, after all, nothing new under the sun.

A few days after Yitzhak Shamir became prime minister, Yoram Aridor's resignation as finance minister presented the new government with its first crisis. Aridor was the third person to leave that office since Likud came to power in 1977. Like the others, Aridor departed leaving the economy in an apparent shambles, with record high inflation and a huge foreign debt. Earlier, Aridor had shown considerable resilience and a flair for survival. The problems may have gone beyond even his capacity.

The time frame of this book is Begin's period as prime minister (1977–1983). It is not so much a record of those years, however, as an effort to plumb the workings of Israeli politics using the Begin years as the major examples. If the task has been done well, the book should offer some explanations of what happened earlier and what is likely to occur in the near future.

Numerous people in Israel and elsewhere helped me gather and interpret the materials presented here. They include academic colleagues, civil servants, friends, and relatives; to attempt a list would risk offending those forgotten. However, Professor David Fellman and Dr. Erich Horn deserve special thanks for having read the entire manuscript. Several chapters derive from materials that appeared in print earlier; thanks are due to the journals and organizations that published them: *Jerusalem Quarterly*, *British Journal of Political Science*, *Public Administration Review*, *The International Journal of Government Auditing*, and Israel's State Comptroller. Thanks also are due to Israel's State Comptroller and to Israel's Authority for Research and Development for financial support that helped me in collecting some of the materials. *Neither of these bodies should be considered responsible for my analyses or conclusions that appear here.* Elizabeth Rubenstein did a splendid job of copyediting.

The dedication is to Varda. Unlike the stereotypical *sabra*, she is sweet on the outside as well as the inside.

CHAPTER 1

Overview

IN THE SPRING OF 1983, ISRAELI TROOPS WERE PA-
trolling throughout the southern half of Lebanon. Ambush
was a constant threat, and the death toll of the operation to
bring peace to the Galilee rose above five hundred. An active peace movement supported Labour party leaders' cries
that the war was ill-conceived and ill-managed. Soldiers
and their families seemed increasingly restive at the prospect of unpleasant and dangerous duty, since the mission
had become as much one of pacifying the chaos of Lebanon
as of protecting Israel from its enemies. Protests against the
war brought counterprotests from government supporters.
The ugliest moment came when a grenade exploded at a
rally of Peace Now (an organization that has pressured the
government to take peace initiatives), killing one of its activists.

At home, the partial strike of physicians went into its
third month. Finance Minister Yoram Aridor refused to

1

meet the doctors' demands for wage increases, citing the need to hold the line on a national wage framework. If he conceded too much to the physicians, Aridor felt, a run of other wage demands would ensue. To escalate their struggle, physicians serving on hospital staffs declared a hunger strike that spread throughout the profession and virtually shut off the major sources of medical care that still functioned. Inflation was already at 160 percent annually, due, in part, to a series of earlier wage increases, and, in part, to new taxes on autos and other imports which were designed to halt the outward flow of money. Exporters of agricultural and industrial products wanted a devaluation of the Israeli shekel in order to make their products competitive with those from other countries, but the finance minister dragged his feet in order to avoid yet another stimulus to domestic inflation. There remained chronic imbalances between government expenditures and revenues.

Amidst the efforts of certain religious leaders and their hundreds of black-frocked yeshiva (religious school) students to halt what they claimed were threats to ancient Jewish burial sites, the archaeologists' summer digging season was about to begin just outside the walls of Jerusalem's Old City. Once the religious issue appeared, other religious figures were impelled to join the chorus, lest they be accused of being less than strictly orthodox. The process of defining who is a Jew according to religious law was another of the religious issues to surface at that time. Using only religious law to define who is a Jew would remove the official designation of "Jew" from many who consider themselves Jewish. For some religious Jews, this is an issue of theological priority. At least some of the nation's religious leaders hoped that these theological issues would disappear from the public arena; they preferred to concentrate their political strength upon the matter of increased financial support for religious institutions.

Yoram Aridor was the third finance minister to serve

in the Begin governments of 1977 to 1983. His two predecessors had resigned when their colleagues in the cabinet
would not support their programs of spending restraint.
Aridor publicly pondered his own resignation. He, too, demanded cuts in the government's budget but found no colleagues willing to sacrifice their programs to benefit the national economy. The minister of education demanded
catch-up pay raises for school teachers, whose salaries had
been determined by a review body some years earlier to
have fallen behind those of fellow workers. Another strike
seemed inevitable if the teachers did not receive more of
what they had been promised. The minister of housing
pressed for more construction in the territories occupied after the war of 1967. He meant to provide homes for the
young adults—many of Asian and African origin—who
were prominent supporters of his party and to continue the
government's policy of settling Jews in the territories. The
universities would not willingly accept further cuts in their
government subsidies. They had just been forced to cut academic staff positions to help finance a court-decreed wage
settlement for faculty members who had struck throughout
the fall term.

Somewhat outside the governmental arena, but still in
the political spotlight, was a dispute in the World Zionist
Organization, a federated body representing Jewish organizations from several dozen countries. Representatives
from Jewish communities abroad—mostly Americans affiliated with the Labour party—would not accept a nominee of
Israel's Likud[1] as head of a major administrative department.

For some citizens, government policies presented immediate personal problems. The country is intimate. Critics
of the government may also be its servants. Some of the
most vocal opponents of the war in Lebanon fought there,
alternating between periods of protest and periods of combat. Some of those who patrol in the cities of Hebron and

Nablus oppose Israeli policies for the West Bank. Supporters of academic freedom from among Israeli university teachers and students are among the soldiers who have used force against the violent demonstrations of Arab high school and university students. One of the reasons for creating government is to have an instrument that will do the unpleasant tasks that citizens prefer not to do themselves. Yet, the distance between Israeli citizens and their government is too close for such a principle to work.

Was this a typical season in Israel? Perhaps. The details change from crisis to crisis, but the fact of several crises crowding one another seems to be constant, as are the elements underlying the crises—limited resources stretched to the breaking point, a confluence of defense and domestic problems, and a number of pressing, expensive, and irreconcilable demands. Conflicts have erupted between Israeli Jews of widely different cultural backgrounds, as well as between secular Jews and the stridently religious. There have been tensions between Israeli Jews and Israeli Arabs.

Israel is a parliamentary democracy. Numerous political parties compete for citizens' support, and many newspapers offer political news and commentary. The economy is a mixture of socialism and capitalism. Much of the economy is tightly controlled by the Finance Ministry and other governmental bodies, but there are opportunities for entrepreneurs in private firms and in the numerous activities that are jointly owned by government and private investors.

The focus of this book is policymaking for domestic activities. Clearly, we cannot be innocent of defense and international affairs. They are prominent among the influences on domestic policy. Yet, our more general task is to identify the distinctive ways by which Israeli politicians, senior civil servants, and citizens cope with difficult problems and imperfect solutions.

ACCOMPLISHMENTS

The domestic challenges and accomplishments of Israel are no less impressive than the country's military record. The desert has been made to bloom. Forests have taken root on slopes made barren by earlier inhabitants. More than 1.6 million immigrants have joined the original population of 900,000. Natural increase combined with immigration to produce a population of 3.3 million Jews and a total population of 4 million in 1981. Many of the newcomers are refugees from extreme poverty and the cruelest of persecutions. They came in desperate need of housing, employment, language training, and other social services. Now, more than thirty-five years since independence and thirty years since mass immigration, Israel's population is usually orderly and productive. Compared to other societies with numerous immigrants, relatively few Israelis have left their country for greener pastures.[2] Israel has created universities, hospitals, orchestras, and museums of world reknown. Several macroscopic indicators sum up the accomplishments of Israel's first years:[3]

1. The population increased from 873,000 at Independence in 1948 to just under 4 million in 1981.
2. The Jewish population increased from 81 percent total at Independence to 84 percent in 1981.
3. The quality of housing improved from 1967, when 4 percent of the Jewish families lived in dwellings with more than four persons to a room while only 15 percent lived in dwellings with less than one person to a room, to 1981, when virtually no Jewish family lived more than four to a room (0.2 percent) and 33 percent lived with less than one person to a room.
4. The incidence of households with telephones increased from 31 percent in 1969 to 66 percent in 1981.

5. The incidence of households with television increased from 2 percent in 1965 to 91 percent in 1981.
6. The incidence of households with private autos increased from 4 percent in 1962 to 34 percent in 1981.
7. The incidence of households with electric refrigerators increased from 34 percent in 1958 to 99 percent in 1981.
8. The incidence of households with washing machines increased from 9 percent in 1958 to 79 percent in 1981.

PROBLEMS

There are indications of severe strains in the Israeli economy. Inflation as measured by the consumer price index (CPI) has been over 100 percent each year since 1980. The shekel has dropped by a factor of more than 4,000 in relation to the U.S. dollar since 1948. In 1948, one Israeli pound (the currency until 1979) was worth four U.S. dollars. Translated to today's currency, this means one shekel would have been worth forty U.S. dollars. A 1980 currency reform created the shekel as the unit of currency, setting one shekel as the equivalent of ten Israeli pounds. As the result of a devaluation in October, 1983, one shekel fell to barely more than one U.S. cent! At the end of 1983, one shekel was worth less than one U.S. cent. Israel is said to have the highest foreign debt per capita of any nation.

Israeli politics always have been noisy and contentious. Some thirty political parties have served in the Knesset (the Israeli parliament) since 1948. None has ever won a majority. Only once has a party received 40 percent of the popular vote. As a result, coalition governments have been the rule, with much squabbling among the factions.

The public scene has been further muddled by important bodies that lie outside the framework of government. Two remnants of the British mandate (1919–1948) are the Histadrut (labor federation) and the Jewish Agency. Both developed to provide social services and government within the Jewish community of British Palestine, and both have retained important roles in independent Israel. The Histadrut and the Jewish Agency are each governed politically with their own constellations of parties and personalities. They play roles in policy-making and service delivery that elsewhere would be within the province of government. There is organizational jealousy and conflict between the officers of different institutions seeking to protect or enhance their organizations, as well as conflict about the nature of social programs.

While it is a given that all countries have problems, Israel's seem particularly acute. If Israel is not the most troubled country in the world, it may be the most troubled country that has continued to govern itself democratically. Israel's tax system takes a higher percentage of the available wealth than that of any other democracy. Some 36 percent of the gross domestic product (GDP) is taken by taxes. The country's military burdens are summed by the 14 to 30 percent of gross national product (GNP) taken by defense expenditures. In other western democracies the comparable figure rarely goes above 5 percent.

COPING

Israelis cope. They make do with less than optimal responses to their difficult environment; they go on with imperfect solutions. Members of the cabinet and other policy-makers cope, as do Israeli citizens. For policy-makers the persistent struggle is to obtain adequate resources. The resource squeeze comes primarily from Israel's unique defense burden. Only rarely—in periods of national emergency—have other countries spent as much on defense as Israel spends every year. Israeli citizens support their military politically; they contribute to it voluntarily, beyond the taxes levied upon them. For example, during a

FIGURE 1.1. Government's Use of Economic Resources

Country	Taken by Government Percentage of GDP
Australia	16
Austria	17
Belgium	17
Canada	20
Denmark	24
Germany	20
Greece	16
Israel	36
Italy	14
Japan	10
The Netherlands	18
New Zealand	15
Norway	18
Portugal	14
Spain	10
Sweden	28
Switzerland	13
United Kingdom	21
United States	18

NOTE: Economic resources are measured by gross domestic product.
SOURCE: *United Nations Statistical Yearbook,* 1979–1980.

FIGURE 1.2. Percentage of GNP Spent on Military

Country	Spent on Military Percentage of GNP
Australia	2.6
Austria	1.3
Belgium	3.2
Canada	2.0
Denmark	2.4
France	3.9
Germany	3.3
Greece	4.7
Israel	24.3
Italy	2.7
Japan	0.9
The Netherlands	3.3
Norway	3.3
Portugal	3.3
Spain	1.8
Sweden	3.4
Switzerland	2.0
United Kingdom	4.8
United States	5.1

SOURCE: Statistical Abstract of the United States, 1980.

one-day campaign in 1982, a military fund dedicated to weapons research and development collected the equivalent of 5 million U.S. dollars. These donations came in wartime, when many of the nation's adult males were called to their reserve units for combat and when a mandatory loan was taking about 7 percent from monthly paychecks, that were already whittled down by normal taxes. Yet another military fund collects donations to provide personal amenities plus sports and cultural facilities for soldiers.

Israel is a welfare state as well as a warfare state. Departments that provide domestic services compete with the military and with each other for shares of national resources. Israel offers free education through high school and provides large subsidies to universities. There are public hospitals in every city and clinics in virtually every neighborhood and small town. Monthly payments are made to all families with children under the age of eighteen, and there are special payments to mothers of the newborn, pensions for the aged, and payments for the unemployed. There is financial aid for industry, agriculture, tourism, and young couples seeking to buy their first home. The government has made commitments to provide additional telephones, begin a second television network, and expand roads and railroads. In 1983, a fifth publicly financed radio network began with music broadcast in FM.

In socialist Israel, a sizable percentage of the work force is employed by government or other public bodies. Israel's extensive public sector includes affiliates of the Histadrut, the Jewish Agency, municipal authorities, hospitals, universities, and companies owned by the government or other public bodies. Employees affiliated with these "public sectors" amount to more than 50 percent of the work force. Wage rates for these employees depend on negotiations with the Finance Ministry. Thus, keeping order on the labor front is a constant problem. Quarterly cost-of-living adjustments to wages compensate for 80 to 90 percent of inflation. Periodic demands are made to catch up with what has been lost in purchasing power despite the cost of living adjustments and to gain an income advantage against later erosion. It is not easy to reward one group of workers without hearing from others. Each is likely to argue that it has fallen even further behind its proper place.

Policymakers who deal with wage negotiations are hindered by the almost totally organized character of Israeli workers, and by the high incidence of public sector employment. There is no extensive free market to define wage standards. Wage settlements depend on pressures from workers' organizations plus the citizens who would be affected by a public sector strike, countered by the efforts of the Finance Ministry to hold the line against a settlement that seems likely to stimulate additional demands from other groups of workers.

Wage settlements include special payments that are made for reasons said to be peculiar to individual groups. Generally, this is a futile device to hold the line against a change in basic salary. Although, for political reasons, "salary" cannot be increased, many groups receive special allowances.

Physicians and nurses receive a special allowance for being on call after working hours. University teachers also claim and receive special payments for being on call. University teachers receive a special allowance for having advanced education. Telephone and electric linemen receive a special allowance for having to work high up on utility poles. Tax inspectors receive an allowance for the stigma of their occupation. (They argue that Israelis are reluctant to befriend a tax inspector or his family for fear of revealing personal details that may lead to an audit.) Postmen receive a "foot allowance" for the pain of having to walk. Laboratory technicians receive what is called an "effort supplement."

Israeli policymakers work in the spotlight of a small theatre with an intense audience. One way they cope with pressure is by making commitments that extend into the future, hoping that things will improve as time for delivery comes nearer. Yet it is just as likely that conditions will worsen. Occasionally workers must strike again for the actual receipt of benefits, after an earlier strike had resulted in the promise of those benefits. Policy-makers also promise more to one another than they can deliver. This occurs regularly with respect to the government budget. The Finance Ministry claims to provide enough of an increase in each year's budget to accommodate the expected inflation. In recent years, however, the ministry's announcement of the expected inflation has been artificially low. When this becomes apparent in the midst of the fiscal year, ministers in charge of the service departments must fight for additional allotments in order to keep their programs alive.

Promising more than could be delivered reached comic proportions in the months before the 1981 election. Yaacov Meridor was a blustery old pal of the prime minister who had been on the fringes of Israeli politics since the War of Independence. He announced a new discovery that would permit a dramatic increase in the energy to be extracted from a barrel of crude oil. His find promised to ease Israel's dependence on unreliable oil producers and to make the country rich from the sale of its patent to others. When the details became public after the election, however, it appeared that the inventor discovered by Meridor had previous experience as a swindler. This time, the inventor had "discovered" a device that had been patented overseas years earlier by another inventor, and was found to be unsuccessful commercially.

Sometimes Israeli policy-makers cope with shortages simply by using the same resources for different purposes. One example is the large number of personnel who work in the civilian sector and serve thirty days or more each year in the military reserves. With virtually full employment and tight budgets, replacement personnel to take the reservists' civilian jobs are almost nonexistent. As a result, a neighborhood's mail may not be delivered for days at a time, classes in school or university go untaught, and work piles up until employees return from the army. This discussion of policy-makers' problems also sheds light on some problems of Israeli citizens. High taxes are one result of Israel's limited resources and the high demands made on her warfare and welfare sectors. Income tax rates reach 60 percent for each shekel earned at a monthly gross income equivalent to about 1,650 U.S. dollars. A value-added tax takes about 15 percent of what Israelis spend on most purchases. In the case of imported autos and appliances, special taxes amount to over 100 percent of the pretax price.

Israel's military burden comes home to most families. Reserve duty has ranged from thirty to ninety days per year since 1973, depending on circumstances. A high incidence of males, ages eighteen to fifty-five, are in combat units for at least part of their military service. Casualty lists reach into one's circle of family or acquaintances. For some, military service carries a moral burden. A few seek to avoid service. For others, the problem is one of balancing distaste for violence with the unrelenting hostility of Israel's antagonists.

Other problems come from public service providers that are either understaffed, undercapitalized or both. People may wait for hours at a Sick Fund clinic, and months for an operation that is not essential. Class sizes reach forty or more in elementary grades; post offices and auto license bureaus are crowded; and, it may take years for a telephone to be installed or weeks for an existing phone to be repaired.

How do Israeli citizens manage? Somewhat like policy-makers, they accommodate themselves to struggle and imperfect solutions. Financially, they may depend on bank overdrafts to meet routine monthly expenses. For something major, there may be gifts or loans from parents and the extended family. Married women tend to work outside the home, and many men find a second job. There is an extensive underground economy, where cash payments escape the tax collector.

A visit to a clinic of the Histadrut's Sick Fund reveals how people cope with crowding. There are queues but they move slowly. Thus, clients act to guard or improve their place in the queue, by periodically signalling their presence to those providing the service. It is common to seek "proteksia," or intercession by a friend on the staff, to insure prompt consideration of one's case.

A tolerance for ambiguity is essential for Israeli policymakers and citizens. Resources are limited, and some promises will not be kept. Struggles are inevitable. Being prepared to struggle, yet remaining civil in the meantime, are prized personal traits.

A resilience to moral conundrum is also helpful. The existential problem of being an Israeli weighs heavily on some, often competing with pride in national accomplishment. Should the government be less aggressive or more forthcoming with respect to the Arabs? Should it be harsher in dealing with overly zealous Jewish nationalists? These problems are made no less easy by their seeming persistence. National security is an obvious problem. The intrasigence of most Arab spokesmen helps to justify a tough Israeli line and assures that the conflict will continue.

For Israelis who tire of the struggle, an exit option exists. The population is cosmopolitan, with a history of personal migration. There are likely to be family members in other countries who provide a magnet. There is much worry about emigration. It is seen as a threat to the zionist ideology, which emphasizes the return of Jews to Zion (Israel). Emigrants raise the fear that Israeli society may crumble from within. In fact, rates of emigration have risen after wars. Recent immigrants are the most likely residents to leave Israel. Some 8 percent of those who arrived between 1969 and 1976 left within three years. However, overall rates of emigration are low when compared to those of other countries that have attracted immigrants, such as

Australia, Canada, New Zealand, or the United States. While Israelis have emigrated at the rate of 20 per 100 immigrants, comparable rates have ranged between 35 and 77 per 100 for the United States, Canada, Australia, New Zealand, and West Germany.[4]

Despite the struggles, Israel seems to work. Pushing for oneself but also respecting national values has long been a feature of the Jewish experience. Rabbi Hillel said it best two millenia ago: "Who am I if I am not for myself? Who am I if I am only for myself?"

How the country works is a story worth telling: it is inherently interesting to those drawn to this country that has attracted so much attention in the world media. This issue is also relevant for those with a scientific interest in techniques for stretching resources or otherwise governing under intense pressures.

One more chapter is devoted to Israel's economic problems and the major features of its government. Chapters 3 through 6 portray problems and accommodations associated with distinctive features of the Israeli society and economy: how the new government of Menachem Begin learned to make economic policy; religion and policy; tactics of budgeting under triple-digit inflation when the essence of the budget (money) has lost its nominal value; and the advantages and problems of supporting governmental activities with voluntary donations. Chapter 7 describes various kinds of government programs that do not work well. Chapter 8 deals with how Israeli citizens cope. Chapter 9 takes an overview of Israeli policy making; it explores the implications of warfare and welfare demands on one another, offers some thoughts on the prospects for peace in the Middle East, and what the effects of peace are likely to be on Israeli society and politics.

CHAPTER 2

Israel's Political-
Economic
Constraints

ISRAEL'S ECONOMY IS HIGHLY MANAGED AND
seemingly unmanageable. It depends on the government,
especially the finance ministry, for a substantial number of
decisions, many of which seem to be wrong. The country's
foreign debt per capita may be the highest in the world. Inflation has been over 100 percent annually each year since
1980. Much of the country's wages and savings rise automatically in response to increases in the cost-of-living index. These linkages are socially appealing but economically
problematic. Inflation is sufficiently harmless so that most
of the time it does not disturb the average voter, but it is
damaging. High inflation confuses the calculations of individual consumers, private entrepreneurs, and government
policy-makers. It hides and excuses ill-conceived decisions
and is partly responsible for pushing the national debt to
record levels. Much new borrowing is used to pay off old
debts, rather than to finance new investments. With each

17

increase in indebtedness, the government may limit its future option to borrow in the event of unavoidable pressures.

The central management of the Israeli economy is reflected by the huge size of the governmental sector. Some 36 percent of the gross domestic product was consumed by government in 1975. In no other Western democracy was the comparable figure greater than 28 percent (Sweden). Typical was a figure of 18 to 20 percent, shown by Australia, Belgium, The Netherlands, the United States, Canada, West Germany, and Norway. Japan and Spain marked the lower end of government consumption, at about 10 percent of gross domestic product.[1]

The high figure for Israel understates the economic involvement of large public bodies in the economy. The Histadrut and the Jewish Agency are technically outside of government. They play important roles as investors and employers and coordinate many of their activities with the government's finance ministry. The Histradut is much more than a collection of labor unions. It owns and manages industries, retail outlets, banks, pension funds, and insurance companies that number among the giants of the country. The Jewish Agency is the Israeli administrative arm of international organizations; it represents Jews in several score countries. Beyond these bodies are corporations that are more nearly private. However, much of the "private" economy is steered along paths chosen by government, and affected by subsidies, regulations, and licenses pertaining to investments, imports, or working conditions.

Although Israel's foreign debt and domestic inflation do not suggest skillful policy making, the country's economic managers must struggle with difficult circumstances. They may be succeeding in keeping the economy from being even more troubled by instability or foreign dependence.

In general terms, Israel scores like one of the poor countries of Western Europe. United Nations figures put its national income per capita ahead of Portugal, Ireland, Greece, and Italy, and slightly behind Spain. Compared to a group of twenty-three Western countries that include Western Europe, the United States, Canada, Japan, Australia, and New Zealand, Israel's national per capita income amounted to 48 percent of the average in 1978. This represents a sharp drop from 1960, when the country's per capita income stood at 83 percent of the same Western average.[2]

The burden of defense is most prominent; its economic weight is actually *understated* by the 14 to 30 percent of gross national product allocated to the armed forces each year from 1973 to 1980. These figures were several times higher than the 1 to 5 percent of gross national product other Western countries allocated to armed forces in the same period. However, several factors are not included in reports of the Israeli government's defense allocations. Only the small outlays for personal compensation and personal maintenance of conscripts are included in the budget documents. Not shown are the economic gains that are foregone by taking virtually all of Israel's young people out of the workforce for the two or three years of conscription, and by drafting most of the males each year for upwards of thirty-days' service in the reserves until they reach their mid-fifties. Also not shown are long-term economic costs of casualties, who typically are young males at the beginning of their productive lives. There is no accounting of the economic transactions that are lost due to Arab boycotts and blacklisting or the fear of war that keeps foreign firms from investing in Israel. Many of the costs for civilian defense are not included in the government's budget; they are incurred by private citizens who must, for example, include reinforced concrete shelters for each dwelling as a condition for receiving construction permits. Likewise, government and private expenditures for stockpiling petroleum, food, and other strategic supplies are not counted as part of defense outlays. Presumably, such costs are higher in Israel than in other countries, where there is not Israel's anticipation of combat.[3]

The government has sought to minimize defense outlays by developing a domestic arms industry. Where this has succeeded, Israel has been able to pay for the arms with shekels. There has been a saving of foreign exchange and even sizable earnings through exports of Israel-produced arms. Locally produced weapons have the added benefit of being tailored to Israel's battlefield requirements. Moreover, locally produced arms are not subject to interruption due to political conditions in the country of origin. However, these optimal solutions are often compromised. High costs of research and development make it attractive to purchase key components or entire weapons systems elsewhere. At times, an offer of financial aid leads Israel to buy overseas, even if the foreign arms are more expensive and no better than those Israel could produce, because a foreign purchase can be financed by a grant or loan that will have less of an immediate impact on domestic inflation.[4]

A problem endemic to Israeli policy makers is that the economy is small and dependent on what happens elsewhere. Israel has always relied heavily on foreign trade. Its ratio of imports to gross national product was 0.70 in 1978; in a group of developing countries, the same ratio was 0.21, and in a group of developed countries it was 0.15.[5] In recent years Israel's earnings from tourism and polished diamonds fell on account of recessions in Western Europe and North America, and its earnings from citrus fruits suffered increasing competition that originated in the low-wage countries of Spain and North Africa.

Immigration has benefitted Israel's economy. The country enjoyed a high growth rate throughout the 1950s and 1960s due partly to infusions of human capital that came via the heavy migrations of 1948 to 1953 and infusions of financial capital from world Jewry and the West German government. Sadly, these economic benefits reflected historic suffering of unmeasurable proportions. Nonetheless, they supported growth rates in gross domestic product per capita of more than five percent annually from 1952 to 1971.[6] Israel's economy also benefits from its high incidence of well-trained professionals and technicians. There is, as well, a fortuitous combination of good soil, modest rainfall, good climate, and sufficient proximity to European markets. The topography of the country provides low-lying areas that are productive in winter and higher elevations that produce in summer.

SLOWER GROWTH PLUS HIGHER DEBT AND INFLATION

The most striking features of the Israeli economy in recent years have been a drop in growth rates, high foreign debt, and record inflation. Growth of gross domestic product per capita dropped to 1.6 percent annually from 1972 to 1981, compared to earlier rates in excess of 5 percent. The annual balance of payments deficits for goods and service imports and exports averaged 2,767 million U.S. dollars from 1970 through 1980, compared to $310 million in the 1950s, and $530 million in the 1960s.[7] Israel's inflation was a modest 9 percent annually from 1968 to 1973. It increased to an annual rate of 36 percent from 1974 to 1977, 51 percent in 1978, 78 percent in 1979, 131 percent in 1980, 117 percent in 1981, and 131 percent in 1982. Midyear reports indicated that the annual rate for 1983 was heading toward 160 percent.

The decline in growth may be due to several factors that are outside the control of Israel's government. Economic slowdown and recession have marked the financial climates of those Western European and North American countries that provide markets for Israeli agricultural and industrial exports, its polished diamonds, and tourism.

Also, Israeli growth statistics of the middle and late 1970s look low when contrasted with the statistics of the 1950s and 1960s, at which times conditions prevailed that are not likely to be repeated. The immigrants who reached Israel by the early 1950s represented, economically, a hoard of potential resources that would pay dividends via training and experience. Those dividends came on stream with annual increases in the productivity of the new labor force. When they reached their peak productivity (about twenty years after they arrived), the immigrants were no longer a source of automatic increases in annual output.[8] And at about the same time, the period of heavy payments by the West German government and by Diaspora Jews ended.

The growth in Israel's balance of payments deficit, and her growing national debt are, in part, a result of the slowdown of the economy's growth and, in part, a reflection of the government's disinclination to tighten the screws too much at home. Among the government and the population, there is little tolerance for unemployment or for the emigration that unemployment may provoke. From 1981 to 1983 the government sought to provide continuing increases in standards of living. It tolerated increased private indebtedness to foreign lenders and the increased import of consumer goods. An increase in government outlays compared to revenues was a major source of heightened inflation.

Israel's inflation is pernicious. It has been harmless to many individuals and therefore tolerable politically. Quarterly cost-of-living adjustments to salaries and wages are universal. Savings schemes, payments for mortgages and other loans, rents, income tax brackets, insurance contracts, municipal taxes and service charges, fines and other court judgments are linked to the consumer price index. While livelihoods and savings are not threatened by Israel's inflation, neither citizens, corporation managers, nor policy-makers can keep track of prices. Consumers cannot recall the constantly changing prices long enough to shop comparatively, which makes sloppiness in financial decisions difficult to avoid. Inflation becomes an easy excuse for those activities of firms and government that cost more than they should. For instance, department heads hide funds for new programs in budgets that are said to grow just because of inflation. Inflation thereby makes it more difficult for the Israeli government to control its own ministries and departments.

The government has trouble dealing with its several economic goals. There is competition between the desire to control inflation and the desire to promote exports, which would thereby minimize the balance of payments deficit. In order to promote exports, industrial and agricultural producers urge more rapid devaluations of the shekel. This would have the effect of making Israeli products cheaper relative to foreign currencies, and therefore more competitive overseas. However, a more rapid devaluation would also make imports more expensive on the Israeli market, and thereby push inflation higher.

From 1981 to 1983 the government tried to pursue a middle course between its concern for exports and its concern for inflation by providing subsidies for exporters (to help them offer lower prices in foreign markets) and keeping the rate of the shekel's devaluation below the rate of inflation. This was something like trying to lose weight slowly without cutting out tasty foods. The result was a spurt of imported consumer goods. Israelis feared that a draconian devaluation would come sooner or later. They imported cars and appliances, took their savings out of company shares, and bought foreign currency. Not only did inflation rise but consumer imports grew along with the balance of payments deficit.

Israel's economic policies were more successful by political than by economic criteria. They recalled the wit who says that politics is a happy science, while economics is a dismal science.[9] Politicians in Israel said "yes" to many claimants, even while economic advisors urged them to be disciplined in allocating resources. This economic posture partially explains the following:

- The government continued to honor heavy resources demands from both warfare and welfare sectors, despite the effect of these demands on deficits in the budget and in the entire economy; the devaluation of the shekel from 0.6 shekels to the U.S. dollar in 1976 to 100 shekels to the U.S. dollar late in 1983 summarizes their impact on the Israeli currency.
- Short-term debt has grown from 18 percent of total obligations in 1974 to 43 percent in 1980.[10]
- Use of foreign loans for private consumption rather than investments has increased.[11]
- Foreign loan commitments have become so large that a substantial portion of new loans must be used to repay the old, thereby decreasing the availability of money for new investments that could add to economic development.

When a new government began in October 1983, it assumed a tougher economic policy. One of its first acts was a devaluation of 23 percent and a commitment to cut government outlays.

POLITICAL AND GOVERNMENTAL CONSTRAINTS

Israel's political and governmental constraints shed light on its economic problems. The country's varied and competitive political groups find their way into governmental mechanisms that defy central direction. No one party or official can build a strong government that can say ''no'' to claimants. There are strong incentives to share resources widely. It is difficult to defend the economy by denying the resource demands of one or another group.

How the Government Works

Up to a point, Israel's government looks like those of other democracies. There is a 120-member parliament, the Knesset, chosen by all citizens eighteen years of age and older in secret ballots. The Knesset chooses the prime minister and other ministers, who govern as long as they retain majority parlimentary support. The president's role is largely ceremonial. He is selected by the Knesset from among the distinguished figures of Israel. His sole political role comes in selecting a potential prime minister when the major parties are closely divided in the Knesset. The work of program implementation is done by professional civil servants, organized into some twenty ministries, plus numerous additional authorities and government companies. The Knesset employs a state comptroller-ombudsman to audit governmental activities and to serve as a recipient of citizen complaints against government authorities. A court system includes initial and appellate courts and a Supreme Court that has ultimate power to rule in disputes between individual citizens or between citizens and their government.

Israel's electoral system is pedantically democratic, with a strict system of proportional representation. Citizens vote for a political party, with each party receiving almost the exact percentage of seats in the Knesset as in the popular vote. The parties themselves select their candidates and array them on a list that numbers from 1 to 120. The party members actually chosen for the Knesset are those from number 1 down to the last number due the party according to its percentage of the vote.

Proportional representation causes a policy-making problem in that it provides support for small parties, each insistent on its own views. Some thirty parties have served in the Knesset since 1948; ten sat following the most recent election in 1981. No party has ever been able to form a majority government; it has always been necessary to accept other parties as coalition partners. Despite the minority status of Israel's ruling parties, most governments have served their allotted terms without having to call elections. The average length of time between elections has been three years and three months, while the legal limit is four years. No Knesset has served less than one year and nine months. Conflict and compromise occur within the cabinet, which includes the prime minister and other ministers. The Knesset is generally a place for noisy debate and eventual ratification of ''deals'' struck in cabinet.

Forming a coalition is an elaborate and sometimes lengthy process. After interviewing the heads of all parties in the Knesset, Israel's president selects as prospective prime minister the person thought most likely to put together a coalition comprising a majority of the Knesset. The prospective prime minister then receives demands from the parties most likely to be coalition partners in the new government. These demands typically include the ministerial appointments the parties would expect as well as the substantive policy issues they would want enacted. Bargaining entails repeated meetings between the prospective prime minister and the heads of other parties, until each partner is satisfied with the total package of commitments. There is a tendency to accept one another's wishes for the support of favored programs, in the grand tradition of political log-rolling. The final agreement among the partners to the 1981 government contained 83 separate items formalized in a document endorsed by all the parties of the coalition.

The pluralistic nature of Israeli politics draws its energy from the pluralistic nature of the society. ''Eastern'' and ''Western'' designate the most prominent social divisions among the Jews, even though the terms are geographically misleading. Some 56 percent of the Jewish population traces its lineage to Eastern societies, which themselves range geographically from Morocco to Afghanistan, and include numerically large and distinctive subgroups like the Iraqis, Yemenites, and the Moroccans themselves. Another 36 percent of the Jewish population is Western in heritage,[12] with internal divisions ranging across heritages as diverse as Argentina and Chile, the United States and Canada, and Western Europe and the Soviet Union.

Another prominent division in the society sets secular against religious Jews. Several parties emphasize the priority of religious issues. The religious parties can count on receiving some 15 percent of the vote. The National Religious party (NRP) has been a member of every government coalition since independence. The NRP or another religious party held enough weight in coalitions to threaten government collapse if it did not get its way on a point considered critical.

There are also conventional ideological divisions in Israel. The Labour alignment, with its socialist traditions, is prominent on the left. Labour ruled and set the tone for Israeli economic and social policy during the first three decades of the country's history. On the right is Likud, with its inclination to free enterprise. Since these great blocs first faced each other, neither has received more than 46 percent nor less than 21 percent of the vote.

Public Bodies

The lack of strong central control by a majority party in the Israeli government is reinforced by other factors on the institutional map. The Histadrut came into being more than twenty years before the Israeli state; it represents almost all workers in matters of wages and working conditions, and operates huge economic enterprises in all sectors of the economy. It amasses capital through Bank Hapoalim (the Workers' Bank), insurance companies, and pension schemes that are among the largest in the country. The Histadrut administers the General Sick Fund, which operates hospitals, clinics, pharmacies, and other health facilities and serves some 80 percent of the population. The Sick Fund depends on government subsidies for much of its resources, and government approval of the tax it charges members. Since 1977 the government has been controlled by Likud, and the Histadrut has remained under the Labour party. While the government and Histadrut have had to make policy together, the incentives to frustrate one another's initiatives have been prominent in the period of divided party rule. The government has pushed for a scheme of national health insurance that would weaken the General Sick Fund. With this fund weakened, Israelis would lose a major incentive to affiliate with the Histadrut, the Labour party would lose, and Likud would benefit. During the physicians' strike in 1983, both the government's health ministry and the Histadrut's General Sick Fund blamed one another for the strike's persistence.

The Jewish Agency is another public body that is older than the government of Israel. It is the Israeli administrative arm of the World Zionist Organization (WZO). WZO brings together Jews from some sixty countries, and collects donations of several hundred million U.S. dollars annually. Much of this money supports social and economic activities in Israel. A principal mission of the Jewish Agency is the recruitment of Jewish immigrants and their integration into Israel. Companies that develop urban housing and agricultural settlements, operate banks, and provide employment in development towns are under the Agency's umbrella. The Jewish Agency plays a role with government ministries in Project Renewal. This is a program to redevelop poor urban neighborhoods and small towns with new building and social programs. The World Zionist Organization and Jewish Agency provide the framework for disputes between Israel and prominent Jews in the diaspora. At times the conflicts are pedestrian: Who should fill administrative posts in the organizations? How should activities between the Jewish Agency and government ministries be coordinated? Other conflicts touch the most profound and sensitive topics in Jewry, such as Israeli responses to U.S. government initiatives for the Middle East or the support for nonorthodox religious movements in Israel given the opposition of the orthodox rabbinate.

Municipal authorities and the large number of government-owned companies are additional actors in policy-making. Although formally under government supervision and control, municipal authorities and government companies can, in practical terms, make their own decisions and present the government with accomplished facts. Both display the competitive defense of institutional terrain inherent in Israeli political style. There seem to be few limits on the quest for resources to finance one's own programs. Mayors approach ministers to obtain extra portions of the national budget for their cities; they are not above skirting the law by arranging for loans with private banks, and then demanding that government help to pay the debts.

Government companies are no more timid than municipal authorities. They develop subsidiaries, alone or in partnership with companies of the Histadrut, the Jewish Agency, or the municipalities.[13] And the subsidiaries create subsidiaries of their own. No one has a firm count of the companies owned directly or indirectly by the government. There are competing definitions of government companies by the Authority for Government Companies (a unit of the Finance Ministry) and the state comptroller. Except for the largest companies or those known to have difficulties, the companies receive scant attention by government bodies responsible for them. Even the most prominent companies, which do attract government's attention, design their own activities and have a considerable impact on the overall economy. Israel Aircraft Industries is the largest employer in the country, with some 20,000 workers. Its products account for an important part of Israel's military hardware and export earnings. Israel Chemicals is in charge of massive activities in the area of the Dead Sea and the Negev. It, too, is an important earner of foreign exchange. El Al is the national air line; in recent years it has recorded losses in the area of 200 million U.S. dollars and has been a source of persistent labor unrest.

The variety of public bodies both lightens and worsens the resource problems of policy-makers. They lighten the burden by spreading the support of public services beyond the government's own taxes and service charges. It may be politically easier to amass resources if more than one body makes demands on the citizenry. Some companies actually make money from profitable goods and services. In the case of Jewish Agency programs, it is especially helpful that substantial resources come as donations from overseas Jews.

On the negative side of multiple public bodies are all the separate organizations and permanent staffs that require support. The sum of governmental bodies plus the Histadrut and the Jewish Agency provide Israel with enormous administrative overhead. The lack of integration between the different public bodies is another serious problem. Each is governed politically, with Labour, Likud, and religious parties; ruling personalities and sometimes parties differ; institutional jealousies prevent a perfect dovetailing of priorities in the best of times and sometimes provoke sharp disputes. Although the government is legally superior to the Histadrut and the Jewish Agency, the prestige and political weight of the Histadrut and the Jewish Agency assure them a degree of autonomy.

Some of the noise that is always present in Israeli politics emanates from the conflicts between the government, Histadrut, and Jewish Agency. There is usually a conflict between the government's ministry of immigration and absorption and the Jewish Agency over their respective responsibilities for bringing immigrants to Israel and providing them with financial assistance and social services. The Histadrut generally seeks higher wage settlements and more generous social benefits than the government's finance minister is willing to endure. With the government under Likud control and the Histadrut under Labour since 1977, the government has acted to weaken the Histadrut by moving important aspects of health-care policy-making from the Histadrut's General Sick Fund into the health ministry. With these numerous bodies, each pursuing their own interests, the government has great difficulty maintaining economic order. Despite a centralization of formal authority, the centrifugal tendency of separate parties, coalition politics, the Histadrut, and Jewish Agency results in deficit, debt, and inflation.

A New Government Learns to Make Domestic Policy

WHEN MENACHEM BEGIN'S LIKUD CAME TO power after the election of 1977, it had no experience at government. The new prime minister and other party leaders had learned the arts of opposition well. They had been opponents for the first thirty years of Israel's history. They were proficient at making speeches and organizing demonstrations against the Labour Party, which had been dominant in all governments since Israeli independence. The election of 1977 proved that Israel was a genuine democracy that could pass the reins of government peacefully to a new ruling party. However, the early years of Israel's new government also showed that governing is a craft not learned in opposition. The period from 1977 to 1980 was a time of learning. The experience of the new government, as described in this chapter, may be joined to the discussion of the previous chapter and thought of as one of the constraints on Israeli policymaking in recent years.

DOMESTIC PROGRAMS: AN OVERVIEW

Sophisticated observers of politics should not expect dramatic changes in the early years of a new government. Declarations of policy intentions are easy, but the actual design and implementation of something new is another story. Governments generally, and democracies in particular, are like supertankers; they change direction only slowly.

Complex structure is one cause of governmental inertia. Few governments are ruled by one person. Even where ministers are members of a single party, there are likely to be disputes about how policy changes will be scheduled and put into effect. Most civil servants carry over in their positions from one government to another. A new government may have trouble finding technically qualified candidates for senior administrative positions among its supporters. This may be especially true of a government that has never held power before. Thus, it becomes necessary to retain holdovers from the previous government. Municipal authorities generally share in the shaping of domestic programs. Mayors and council members are responsible to their local electorate, and may remain in office for some years after a new political wave has brought about changes at the national level.

Established programs have lives of their own. Because clients and staff members tend to oppose too many rapid changes, new decisions are usually made incrementally, to be added or subtracted from what exists. If major change does occur, it may be apparent only years after the fact, as a result of repeated steps in a certain direction. The first step may be small and deliberately disguised to minimize opposition.

Even if new policies are pursued, the competition that prevails in democratic societies helps to obscure the reality

CHAPTER 3

of change. Parties compete on post hoc analyses as well as on campaign promises. Opponents seek to minimize the success of government programs. Complex conditions also frustrate simple assessment. What proportion of an upturn in an economic indicator is due to the policy of a new government, to the groundwork laid by its predecessor, or to extraneous events in the national or world economies? Seldom are there clear answers to such questions, especially when opposing parties compete with their own experts, data, and interpretations.

The lack of priority given to domestic programs is an additional factor that worked to inhibit policy changes from 1977 to 1980. Unlike the citizenry in other democracies, Israelis concern themselves more often with foreign than with domestic policy. The explanation is obvious, given the beleaguered nature of the country. Menachem Begin's government was likely to be especially concerned with matters of defense and international relations. Throughout his political life, Begin was preoccupied with the dark side of Jewish history and the need to protect Israel from hostile outsiders. As prime minister, he gave highest priority to thickening Jewish settlement in the territories occupied after the 1967 war, relations with the great powers and Arab neighbors, defense against terrorism, and military resources. As a consequence, little time or energy remained for the details of economic management, education, health, or other domestic issues.

No analysis of Israeli policy-making could find that the Begin government failed to innovate. The record of negotiations with Egypt was a landmark in Israeli history. Begin's government was the first to achieve a signed peace with an Arab neighbor, notably, the most powerful of Arab countries. The negotiations with Egypt required that the prime minister and his colleagues change their thinking drastically about Jewish settlements in the area demanded by that country. Paradoxically, the striking character of Israeli international relations in the first years of the Begin government may have retarded policy-learning in domestic fields.

Two studies looked at Begin's early domestic policy-making.[1] Both found that new ventures were more innovative in appearance than in fact. Much that was advertised as new were simply extensions, embellishments, or repackagings of previous activities. The government could more readily give more resources to an existing program and change its scope or its name than develop a program that was truly new.

LEARNING ECONOMIC POLICY-MAKING

The ebb and flow of economic policy from 1977 to 1983 provides detailed insights into the learning of a new government. It is helpful to describe three distinct periods in economic policy-making, more or less corresponding to the tenures of the three men who served as finance ministers. While we deal exclusively here with economic policy-making in Israel, a more general message may be found that applies to the policy-learning of new governments elsewhere.

Period I: Symbolic Policy Changes

Less than two months after coming to office in 1977, Simcha Ehrlich, Begin's first minister of finance, explained to the Knesset that there had not been enough time for the government to change economic policy;[2] hence, adjustments to the budget that had been inherited from the Labour government were offered. Three months later, in November 1977, the same finance minister announced a "New Economic Policy" that included a free-floating currency and authority for Israeli citizens to hold unlimited amounts of foreign currency. These were innovations since Israelis had always faced rigorous currency controls. Liberalism (or limited government control) was the theme of the New Economic Policy, in keeping with Ehrlich's Liberal party affiliation. There would be a general reduction of government's role in the economy, government companies would be sold to the private sector, subsidies reduced, and market competition given a new importance. Reduced government spending would help to stabilize prices. In January 1978, Ehrlich set a 13 percent inflation target, to be achieved by fiscal year 1980.[3]

Ehrlich's implementation of liberalism hardly lived up to his proclamations. One failure was in the aspiration to sell government companies to private investors. The Begin government may have sold off fewer company shares than its Labour predecessor. Israelis' rights to hold foreign currency were tightened significantly after the New Economic Policy was proclaimed, and again after the program went into effect. While the value of the currency theoretically floats in response to supply and demand under the liberal regime, the Bank of Israel effectively sets the rate of exchange via its currency trading.[4] That rate moved steadily downward—from 0.24 U.S. dollars in late 1974 to less than 0.01 at the end of 1983 (taking account of the replacement of the pound by the shekel as the unit of currency). In contrast to Ehrlich's target of 13 percent, inflation reached 131 percent in 1980. By comparing this inflation rate to the 36 percent rate of the Labour party's last years (1974 to 1977), we can see the meaning of *symbolic* policy changes.

Period II: Coming of Age: Enactment and Implementation of Distinctive Policy Innovations

Implementation was the key word in the new government's passage from Period I to Period II. The latter marks an end to mere innovative declarations and the beginning of relatively new actions. The Begin government did not clearly and all of a sudden reach this second stage. It was a process that seemed to require the appointment of trusted partisans to quasi-political, quasi-technical positions that for years had been the sole preserve of the Labour party. Prominent here are directors general of the ministries, governor of the central bank, director of state finance, and director of the budget department in the finance ministry.

The first signs of Period II appeared during the tenure of Begin's second finance minister, Yigal Horvitz, appointed in 1979. Horvitz not only declared war on inflation, but implemented severe and distinctive programs to combat it. Annualized inflation declined from 168 percent in the fourth quarter of 1979 to 96 percent in the first quarter of 1980.[5] However, Horvitz was too distinctive for his own good. He was not willing to compromise with colleagues who demanded a softening of spending restraints for their programs. Horvitz and his policy departed the government in January 1981.

Period III: Maturity

Period III reversed much of Period II's emphasis on new and distinctive accomplishments—accomplishments that had been too distinctive. They threatened the political future of the Likud government. Unemployment was up, and living standards, down. Period III was the era of Begin's third finance minister, Yoram Aridor. He took office in the period before the 1981 election and helped to turn Likud's electoral image around. Aridor replaced Horvitz's austere postures with populist policies, such as cutting import duties and cheapening the price of autos, color television, and appliances. As part of the government's coalition agreements with religious parties, substantial outlays flowed to schools and other institutions of the religious parties. And, as part of the government's policy to expand settlements in the occupied territories, substantial funds (largely off-budget) flowed to the construction of new towns. For the first time, the image of settlers in the territories changed from one of a few highly motivated, religious or nationalist families willing to live under trying physical conditions to a mass of young, middle-income families seeking homes made affordable by subsidized purchase prices and mortgages.[6]

The commitment to economic liberalization was gone.[7] Period III's themes were coping, business as usual, and taking opportunistic advantage of circumstances. The period's posture toward inflation was symptomatic of these themes. Inflation was not considered a desirable condition. However, after Horvitz's harsh campaign against it, inflation came to be viewed as something that was unbeatable without antagonizing too many industrialists, workers, and beneficiaries of government programs. The government learned to make the best of an undesirable situation. For instance, relying on loans obtained by contractors to finance off-budget housing in the occupied territories contrasted with earlier declarations about proper budgeting made by Finance Minister Ehrlich.[8] However, the budget evasion managed to get housing constructed and people moved to the occupied territories, which was in keeping with government policy.

Many aspects of Period III seemed inevitable. If it was not the complete capitulation of a new government to unbeatable forces of environmental constraints and its own political aspirations, it was something close to that. Period III was a time marked by policy emphases distinct from those of the earlier Labor government. However, the true innovations may be difficult to discern amidst similarities to the past and opportunistic accommodations to present realities. In Period III, the Begin government seemed to face the limits of its own power. It wanted to be good to the people, and it did so by sacrificing the aspirations of Period II to cut government spending and put the economy in order.

The struggle between difficult and easy policies of Periods I through III—with the easy generally winning the upper hand in Period III—is a condition that finds ready explanation in the general literature of political science and in the details of Israeli politics. Governments worldwide tend to take an easy course of action. Reformers must cope with the sticking power of existing commitments to jobholders and service recipients. Bargaining between elites of different perspectives dilutes bold statements. Yet, there are likely to be pressures within a new government to do something new immediately. These pressures give rise to appealing devices of symbolic proclamation and cosmetic policy changes. These are easier than substantive program changes. Newcomers to office can claim credit for doing something new, without dealing with many of the factors needed to assure the actual delivery of something new.[9]

Pressures for innovation may be especially great in a ruling party that has always been in opposition. Period I and Period II represent the first efforts and frustrations of parties that must learn to govern. Period III reflected the new government's recognition of some limits and realities of power.

Subsidies

The government's efforts to lessen subsidies provide an archetypal illustration of the frustrations encountered on the road from policy declarations to political reality. At various points in their tenures, all of Begin's finance ministers declared themselves in favor of reducing the subsidies carried over from thirty years of Labour's socialist rule. The noise was shrillest in periods I and II. Begin's first two finance ministers took the clearest steps to cut subsidies. The distinctiveness of Period III was an opportunistic acceptance of subsidies as one tool of economic policy.

Period I Finance Minister Ehrlich announced the first subsidy cuts less than a month after the Likud-dominated government came to power. As a result, fuel costs increased between 25 and 33 percent, and bus tickets increased by 25 percent.[10] Another 60 percent in subsidy cuts were proposed in 1978 government budget discussions.[11] At various times in the tenures of Finance Ministers Ehrlich and Horvitz, finance ministry spokesmen signaled their opposition to special aids for the poor as a result of subsidy cuts and price rises. During one month in 1977, when price increases averaged more than 12 percent, a deputy minister of finance stated that the effects of the policy change would be considered, and compensations for the poor decided, only sometime in the future.[12] Late in 1979, Finance Minister Horvitz offered increased child payments of 4 percent, during a wave of subsidy cuts that raised the prices of some items from 25 to 100 percent.[13]

Despite the attitude favoring liberalization and subsidy cuts, both Ehrlich and Horvitz had to live with compensations for the poor that tempered the effects of such cuts. Finance minister Ehrlich retreated from the policy of subsidy cuts one month after taking office, and two weeks after declaring his first cuts in subsidies. He cited the need to preserve labor peace by coming to agreement with the Histadrut.[14] He could just as truthfully have spoken of the need to keep the peace within the government coalition. David Levy advocated continued subsidies for basic foodstuffs and public transportation, and compensations for the poor whenever subsidy cuts were implemented. Levy was the most prominent spokesman for lower-income, Asian and African Jews in Begin's governments; he began as minister of immigration, and was promoted to minister for housing and construction and deputy prime minister.

Subsidies may actually have increased overall during Periods I and II, despite the contrary efforts of the finance ministers. The budget for 1980 originally included subsidies only for bread and public transportation. During the course of deliberations, the government added subsidies on frozen poultry, margarine, cooking oil, fuel, water, and animal feed.[15] One study showed that government subsidies of public transportation increased from 27 percent in 1973-1974 (Labour government), to 73 percent in 1980-1981.[16] As part of a budget supplemental passed in 1981-1982, the figure indicated for all subsidies increased from 6 to 16 billion shekels.[17] Further subsidies continued indirectly, as government bodies delayed or diluted price increases for electricity, fuel, postal services, financial credits, and university tuition.[18]

On occasion Aridor, the Period III finance minister, indicated his inclination to cut subsidies.[19] However, he seemed equally at ease with continuing or increasing them, depending upon which was politically expedient. Aridor accepted the argument that it was cheaper to subsidize certain goods than to compensate for subsidy cuts through increases in wages and welfare payments triggered by cost-of-living adjustments.[20] During 1982, subsidies for bread amounted to 170 percent of the price paid by the consumer; for milk products, 85 percent; for eggs, 65 percent; and for frozen poultry, 70 percent. Fuel prices were allowed to increase only 67 percent in 1981-1982, while prices, generally, inflated by more than 100 percent.[21]

Inflation

High inflation was the most prominent economic feature of the Begin years. Price increases averaged 36 percent annually in the last three years of Labour Party rule, and 102 percent in the first five years of Likud rule. At various times the annual rate, as projected from month to month, went over 200 percent.[22] Such figures may be viewed as reflecting economic changes made by the Begin government. There is no evidence, however, that inflation was the chosen goal of economic policy-makers.

Israel's inflation is caused by a combination of events external to her borders and by side effects of government policies. These events and side effects include: the spurt of international oil prices in 1979; the costs of complying with the Camp David peace treaty with Egypt, especially the withdrawal of military and civilian locations from the Sinai; the spurt of domestic prices that followed the New Economic Policy of 1977, with its 43 percent devaluation of Israeli currency and price jump on imported goods and services; price increases in basic commodities and public transportation that followed cuts in government subsidies; the comprehensive system of price linkages that increased wages, mortgage payments, and many other cost-of-living items; the unwillingness of government ministers to sacrifice or compromise their own programs in the face of efforts by finance ministers to make significant cuts in the budget; policy commitments of high priority, such as expanding settlements in the West Bank, and increasing government support of religious education; and the persistence of government spending over government revenue.

Each of Begin's finance ministers identified price stability as a major goal. Their activities differed greatly, however, in keeping with the general characters of Period I, Period II, and Period III. With respect to inflation, the periods might be labeled: *Bold proclamations, ineffectual behavior; All-out war;* and *Acceptance of high inflation as a given and coping within that framework.*

Simcha Ehrlich approached the task of finance minister as a good member of the Liberal party. He declared it his intention to minimize the government's role in the economy. His more doctrinnaire deputy, Yhezkl Flumin, occasionally spoke as if he thought it possible to extract the government entirely from the economy! Ehrlich declared himself to be solidly against inflation. In January 1978 (with inflation running at an annual rate of 31 percent) he set as his target an inflation rate of 13 percent for 1980.[23] In reality the overall 1980 rate became 131 percent, and it reached 250 percent (annualized) in the month of October. Ehrlich himself contributed to the inflation, albeit unwittingly. His liberalization of controls over foreign currency, and his massive devaluation (perhaps to help the exports of his party's industrialists) spurred sharp increases in domestic prices. His cuts or elimination of subsidies further boosted domestic prices, all of which fed back into inflation via cost-of-living adjustments. Once inflation reached triple digits, the government acceded to the Histadrut's demand for more frequent cost-of-living adjustments; these adjustments came quarterly instead of semiannually. Ehrlich seemed to weaken visibly under the torrent of demands from his own party to hold the line of true liberalism, and stronger demands from other coalition partners to make spending concessions for the clients of almost every government ministry. Ehrlich left the Finance Ministry in late 1979. Since his departure, the Liberal party has not succeeded in promoting one of its own to the post of finance minister.

Yigal Horvitz came to the finance ministry as a tough-talking industrialist-politician who would be strong where Ehrlich had pussy-footed. His motto became ''I don't have any,'' the stock response when ministers sought money. He was the only one of Begin's finance ministers willing to create unemployment among wage earners as part of his war against inflation.[24] He regarded it a sign of success that living standards actually declined in 1980.[25] While he presided over the record high inflation of 131 percent in 1980, he claimed to have reduced the projected annual rate (estimated on the basis of quarterly data) from 180 percent when his predecessor left office.[26] For all his bluster, Horvitz was also a prisoner of political realities. His program found support in public opinion polls, but he could not resist the demands of his government colleagues for more spending in behalf of their projects.[27] The prime minister generally backed compromise, which resulted in tactical and strategic losses for the finance minister. During a Knesset discussion of the economy in November 1980, an opposition member noted that Horvitz had projected that his ministry would pursue an anti-inflationary policy and absorb 3.5 billion pounds from the economy. It was apparent that the government had pursued inflationary policies, however, and overspent its revenues by 58 billion pounds (860 million U.S. dollars).[28]

Horvitz ultimately left office because he could not accept the compromises that were demanded by his colleagues. The precipitating event was a protracted dispute over the wages of primary and secondary school teachers. A commission of inquiry found serious erosion in the teachers' salaries and recommended catch-up improvements. When the education minister demanded money, Horvitz's response was "I don't have any." The prime minister wanted more for the teachers than Horvitz felt possible. Thus Horvitz left office in January 1981.[29]

Yoram Aridor's motto, in explicit contrast to Horvitz's, was said to be, "I have some." Aridor was a political creature under Prime Minister Begin. Compromise, and the exploitation of opportunity were part of Aridor's public nature; he was the least ideological and the most adaptable of Begin's finance ministers. Bargaining marked his Period III strategy with respect to inflation.

Aridor asserted that there is no six-day war in economics.[30] This statement is one indication that Aridor enjoyed some conflicts. He provoked his longtime antagonist, the general secretary of the Histadrut, by publicly offering cost-of-living adjustments that seemed more generous than those supported by the Histadrut.[31] He was less bothered than his predecessors by the theatrics of contending ministers.[32] Aridor abandoned the strident campaigns against subsidies. He viewed the continuation of subsidies as less inflationary than the spiraling price and wage increases that are generated by subsidy cuts. His populist policies of reducing import duties on selected consumer goods helped Likud win a second term in the 1981 elections, and he proved to be a survivor of intragovernmental squabbles until the early days of the Shamir government. Standards of living increased during his tenure. Aridor served for thirty-one months as Begin's finance minister, compared to Horvitz's fourteen. Aridor's detractors asserted that he funded his success by ill-advised reliance on foreign bank loans and U.S. government aid.[33] And, in fact, there was a substantial increase in Israel's foreign debt during his tenure. His resignation came dramatically, at a cabinet meeting that rejected his proposal for economic repair. The finance minister who was flexible for thirty-one months seemed to have reached his limit.

Accomplishments

Period III featured a struggle between innovation on the one hand and compromise on the other hand. Up to now, we have emphasized the ascendency of compromise in Period III. What of the innovations? Three lines of policy development emerged from the general picture of protracted bargaining. Two of them were positive, in that they awarded substantial resources to programs favored by the Begin coalition. A third was negative, in that it reduced resources that had customarily gone to a sector outside of the Begin camp.

Religious parties held a balance of power in both Begin governments. More than that, their traditionalist Jewish values were to the prime minister's personal liking. The religious parties received numerous favors, for having joined the coalition.[34] Prominent among these was substantial funding for religious institutions. More than any other sector, the Ministry of Religions's budget moved upward in real terms. During 1981–1982, the ministry's budget increased by 390 percent in real terms, while almost every other ministry's budget declined.[35] And in Aridor's initial budget for 1982–1983, Religions was the only ministry to enjoy real growth.[36] Further spending for religious purposes was included in the budgets of other ministries, such as Education.

A second area to benefit from a substantial flow of resources was settlements, especially in the territories occupied as a result of the 1967 war. A distinctive policy innovation was the offering of generous housing terms to young couples. (The typical settler during the Begin years was motivated by an affordable home, rather than by nationalist or religious zeal.) The government's hope was to attract thousands of families to the territories, thereby ensuring that substantial areas would remain in Jewish hands. The extent of the financial flow for this purpose is elusive, insofar as much of it was conducted off-budget, via loans obtained by housing companies. Among the economic consequences of the latter policy was a substantial increase in debt, some part of which was held by foreign banks; and a spurt of government-inspired activity for the construction industry.

The collective agricultural sector (kibbutzim) was distinctively on the outside of the Begin coalition. The kibbutzim are the historical preserve of the Labour party. On some settlements, over 95 percent of the members voted against Begin. Policywise, agriculture suffered. Begin's first agricultural minister was Arik Sharon, better known for his earlier military career and later tenure as defense minister. During his period as agriculture minister, Sharon concentrated on building settlements in the occupied territories. The second agriculture minister was Simcha Ehrlich, who earlier had had a stormy two and one-half years as Begin's first finance minister. Neither Sharon nor Ehrlich invested much of their spirit in agricultural policy, per se, and neither fought prominently to assure Agriculture's share of the budget. Agricultural and Labour commentators are sharply critical of Begin's policies; they contrast them with the Labour-Zionist traditions of bringing forth produce from the land. Annual government investment in agriculture actually fell during Begin's years, for the first time in Israel's history. At one point, the agricultural sector was threatened further by the imposition of a value-added tax on its produce. Israeli products did not prosper in competitive and depressed international markets. Kibbutz spokesmen commented bitterly about Jewish farmers leaving the land to invest in a stock market favored by the Likud government.[37]

ELECTIONS AND POLICY CHANGES

Since democratic theory holds that elections are a primary influence on the content of policy, an important question is whether the 1977 election brought about new policies in Israel.[38] The Likud government sought to change the economic policies of preceding Labour governments. In general, however, the policy changes actually implemented differed from those proclaimed. There was much protracted bargaining and compromise. The result was that the Likud government continued many of the policies developed during the long rule of the Labour party. The domestic-economic infrastructure and international influences that impacted upon Israel's policy options remained largely as they were. The Histadrut continued to be a potent force in domestic affairs, and remained under the Labour party's rule. Begin's governments were coalitions that had to find paths acceptable to contentious partners.

The responses of Begin's economic policy-makers to these challenges fit a pattern of three periods. In the first period, more or less contiguous with the tenure of Finance Minister Simcha Ehrlich, there were bold proclamations. For some of what was proclaimed—like the general liberalization of the economy—the results were much diluted from the proclamations. The massive devaluation of the currency that came as part of the liberalization package brought with it a stimulus to inflation that can only be described as a negative side effect. Ehrlich suffered from not having had a cadre of personnel who were both loyal partisans and skilled technocrats. The Israeli economy still suffers from some miscalculations attributable to Ehrlich's policies.[39]

Period II began during the tenure of Finance Minister Yigal Horvitz; his reign was distinctive and colorful. Horvitz did what he could to cut subsidies and hold down government spending. He viewed labor mobility and unemployment as acceptable costs of anti-inflationary policy, and he boasted of having reduced Israelis' standard of living. Horvitz did not know when to compromise, however, which is one reason why he did not survive.

Yoram Aridor served for thirty-one months as Begin's third finance minister. His tenure had the look of mature adaptability to economic challenges and political reality. He pursued economic goals, like a restraint of further growth in the rate of inflation and the funding of substantive policies that were given high priority by the government coalition. However, he also pursued his own and his government's political survival. He contributed to the political business cycle with a preelection wave of selective tax reductions on consumer goods. There was not much ideological content in his public remarks. His approach to subsidies was practical—they are often cheaper than the consequences of cutting them. His budget strategy was marked by continuous bargaining throughout the fiscal year, much of it outside the public spotlight. For a while he held the line against further growth in the inflation rate. One of the ways he did this was by increasing foreign borrowing. When Menachem Begin resigned, Yoram Aridor served for a few days as finance minister to prime minister Yitzhak Shamir. At this point the weight of inflation and foreign debt had come to the government for discussion.

Looking at Yoram Aridor from a point several months

into the career of his successor, we find that Period III placed too much emphasis on political convenience and not enough on economic realities; the Israeli public had come to distrust the government's capacity for economic survival. Fear of the shekel's imminent devaluation turned to panic in the stock market. Individuals sold shares denominated in shekels in order to buy foreign currency. A new finance minister—Yigal Cohen-Orgad—came to office committed to economic orthodoxy and tough political decisions. The pendulum seemed to swing back in the direction of Period II's finance minister, Yigal Horowitz. However, the problems that had limited Horowitz's success continued: members of the government coalition in charge of the spending ministries were not eager to sacrifice too many of their own priorities for the general goal of economic well-being.

In this chapter I have not attempted to generalize beyond the issue of economic policy-making in Menachem Begin's government. Nevertheless, the fit between the latter and the findings and expectations drawn from the literature of political science suggest a more general pattern. A new government can proclaim bold new policies with relative ease. Implementation, however, is another matter. To actually deliver something innovative, newcomers to power may have to put their cadres into the positions that provide leverage over policy, and learn to devise programs that will operate as intended. Yet, programs that are too boldly innovative may doom their creators to a short political life. At the other extreme, too little regard for economic orthodoxy may risk the loss of citizens' credibility. A mature new government would seem to require a delicate combination of technical skills and a sense of political reality.

Domestic policy learning may come more quickly when a government is not preoccupied with foreign policy. Part of the Israeli condition is a preoccupation with national security, for which the country may have paid a high price in her slow learning of domestic policy-making.

CHAPTER 4

Religion and Politics

THERE HAVE ALWAYS BEEN RELIGIOUS ISSUES IN Israel's politics. From the outset, when independence was achieved in 1948, religious and secular leaders differed as to whether the state should be declared at all, and if so, how the issue of the Almighty should be treated in the formal declaration. The compromise included allusions to both religious and nonreligious antecedents of modern Israel and the use of a name for the Almighty that could satisfy both the religious and secular camps. Since then religious issues have erupted from time to time with sufficient force to topple governments. Members of the National Religious party voted against their Labour-led government coalition in 1977 to protest a military ceremony that was held too close to the onset of the Sabbath, thereby providing a major push toward the government's collapse.[1]

Since Menachem Begin and his Likud-led coalition came to power in 1977, religious issues have been prominent. There has also been a change in the pecking order of religious parties. A new driving force distinguishes itself in the character of the issues it raises. Agudat Israel seems to be challenging the maintenance of the *status quo.* The principle of status quo had developed to govern religious policy, by preventing significant movement in either pro- or antireligious directions. By preventing change, both religious and secular politicians sought to keep sensitive issues below the flash point of political explosion. Since 1977, however, numerous secular Israelis have felt that their state is under siege from within. Often they exaggerate the success of religious politicians. Like their secular competitors, religious parties endure compromise and frustration. Religious politics in Israel include the theological and political rivalries between Jewish religious communities, as well as conflicts between religious and secular Jews. Also, the success of the religious parties has varied significantly from one field of policy to another.

HISTORICAL BACKGROUND: RELIGIOUS AND ZIONIST

For the first twenty-nine years of Israel's history, the National Religious party (NRP) set the tenor of religious politics. It held ten to twelve places in each 120 member Knesset and was a perennial partner in coalition governments. Leaders of the National Religious party accepted and supported the state. Their sons generally serve in the military instead of using their option of exempting themselves because they were students in a religious institution. The daughters of NRP members often opt for national service in one or another social field, or accept conventional military service. In families belonging to other religious movements, young women tend to opt out of both national service and the army.

At several points, from 1948 to 1977, the demands of the NRP stood apart from those of secular parties. As guardian of the faith within the different government coalitions, NRP sought to preserve the status quo of religious standards against the encroachment of secular interests. It opposed the legitimization of secular marriage and divorce and sought to limit work on the Sabbath and religious holidays, especially in public institutions. On more than one occasion, the NRP's insistence on a point of religious law caused a government crisis.

With Israel's acquisition of the West Bank, the Golan Heights, and the Sinai as a result of the 1967 war, the NRP's religious Zionism supported an active settlement policy. Party activists urged a return of Jews and the perpetuation of Jewish rule in all of Israel under Jewish control. The religious nationalist movement, *Gush Emunim*, developed partly due to efforts of NRP members.

The first Begin administration from 1977 to 1981, proved to be both a high point for the NRP and its turning point for the worse. Prime Minister Menachem Begin expressed his support for religious as well as nationalist values, and lent enthusiastic approval to an active settlement program in the occupied territories. At the same time, however, the NRP minister of religions, Aharon Abuhatzera, was sinking into the mud of criminal charges concerning his mishandling of funds. He charged that the European Jewish NRP establishment failed to support him because of his Moroccan background, and he established Tami, a party that made both ethnic and religious appeals. A new nationalist party, Tahiya, emerged to oppose the return of Sinai settlements to Egypt that resulted from the Camp David agreements of 1978. Tahiya won the votes of many of NRP's followers, people who had originally supported Gush Emunim. Tami captured three seats in the 1981 elections, Tahiya another three, and NRP's strength dropped from twelve to six. NRP also faced competition from the religious right wing during the 1977 to 1981 government.

Agudat Israel joined the governing coalition for the first time since 1951, and asserted its initiatives on religious policy.

HISTORICAL FOREGROUND: RELIGIOUS AND NOT QUITE ZIONIST

Agudat Israel is now the prominent party in religious politics. Its ascendance over the NRP is due to several factors: its more stridently and uncompromisingly religious character; its success in disciplining its various factions, at least with respect to their public activities; the taint of scandal and the split in NRP surrounding the trial and conviction of the former minister of religions; and the sharp decline in NRP's parliamentary strength after the 1981 elections. Agudat Israel dominates religious policy-making far out of proportion to its four seats in the Knesset against the six of the NRP.

Agudat Israel comes from a stream of religious Judaism that was nurtured in the diaspora and has made peace with the Jewish state belatedly and only partly. More extreme groups from the same stream, like Neturei Karta, have yet to accommodate themselves to the state.[2] These extremists are even more otherwordly than Agudat Israel. Their perspective is fixed entirely on study and personal behavior according to sacred writings and interpretations they view as authoritative. To the most extreme of them, any secular Jewish state that predates the coming of the Messiah is sacrilege. They prefer to live in, and make their accommodations to states governed by gentiles. An extreme few have expressed their preference for a Palestine governed by the Palestinian Liberation Organization (PLO) rather than an Israel governed by Jewish political parties. Agudat Israel participates in the Jewish state even while it is not entirely free of antagonism toward that state. The party has had representatives in every Knesset; after 1977 it played a role in the government coalition and chaired key committees in the government and the Knesset.

Comments made by Agudat Israel in its own press reveal a combination of certainty about its monopoly of religious leadership and a disdain for other religious parties, along with some ambivalence about its role in the state. At times it is too otherwordly for its own good. It hesitates to achieve some of its key objectives because it is reluctant to give state officials more power in religious affairs.

The daily newspaper of Agudat Israel, *Hamodea* (literally translated "The Announcer") is clearly the organ of a political movement. It knows no boundaries between news and editorials. All of its material on national politics is the terrain of party polemicists. There are distinctions between friends, enemies, and allies of the moment. The leaders of various factions within Agudat Israel are treated with the greatest respect, as illustrated by words of reverence such as *genius, our leader, teacher, and rabbi,* that are bestowed on them by their followers. There are frequent assertions of unity among the party's factions. Sometimes, however, *Hamodea* hints at the severe intraparty conflicts that are detailed in the pages of competing newspapers.

The treatment of Prime Minister Begin by *Hamodea* revealed the ambivalence toward secular leaders that is felt by many figures in Agudat Israel. Often the prime minister was portrayed as supportive of religious interests and as sharing personally in the pleasures and tribulations of an observant Jew. Several times *Hamodea* reported the prime minister's story of refusing to sit for a Latin exam given many years earlier on a Sabbath in Poland, and thereby suffering in his grades. Yet other articles assert that the Likud, including Begin, is secular. Its members are said to be, at best, "traditional Jews," without the deep and uncompromising attachment to religious law that is expected within Agudat Israel. Such articles indicate that Agudat Israel's alliance with Begin and other secular Jews is likely to be temporary. In time, Likud will treat Agudat Israel as something of secondary importance in the face of its secular priorities.[3]

Hamodea also reveals the distance that Agudat Israel prefers to maintain between itself and religious figures more closely identified with the Zionist state. Its comments about the National Religious Party are occasionally contemptuous. It asserts that the NRP represents a different world, which does not share the values of Agudat Israel.[4] The newspaper protests "antireligious" policies pursued by NRP-controlled ministries. It was caustic in its comments about the minister of education and culture, Zebulin Hamer, for not having stood firm with Agudat Israel against the archeologists' violation of ancient Jewish graves.[5] It criticized the minister of interior (also responsible for police and prisons) for police brutality against religious people who protested the sacrilege of archaeologists,[6] and for not permitting prisoners the opportunity to live a fully religious life during their confinement.[7] When NRP-allied settlers were protesting their forced withdrawal from northern Sinai, *Hamodea* aligned itself with the government. It asked why self-professed religious members of *Gush Emunim* did not appear at demonstrations on behalf of truly religious causes like the sanctity of gravesites or the prohibitions of abortions and autopsies. The newspaper supported the sanctity of contracts (the peace treaty with Egypt), and the priority to be given peace over territory. It considered the spilling of blood for political purposes to be sacrilege.[8]

The organizational structure of Agudat Israel helps to explain its politics. The building blocks of the party are orthodox religious communities. Each is inward-oriented, with commitments to its own schools and rabbis; at the same time each also participates in the larger party framework.[9] One apocryphal story expresses the tensions among the orthodox communities. When asked which other religion he considered closest to Judaism, the rebbe (leader) of one community within Agudat Israel is said to have replied, "Chabadism," which is another orthodox Jewish movement.

The rabbis affiliated with Agudat Israel rule autonomously on matters of religious law for their communities. Agudat Israel looks with some suspicion at the organization of the Chief Rabbinate. It is part of the state and might impose its will on the constituent communities of Agudat Israel. Moreover, the Chief Rabbinate and the Ministry of Religions are creatures of the National Religious party. At times Agudat Israel has supported an increase in the authority of the Chief Rabbinate. It would like the Chief Rabbinate, rather than the Ministry of Education and Culture, to regulate the activities of archaeologists. At other times, however, Agudat Israel would rather sacrifice a point of religious law than give more authority to the Chief Rabbinate. Some leaders of Agudat Israel urged retreat on the prominent issue of defining *who is a Jew* according to religious law, out of fear that the Chief Rabbinate would be authorized to administer the provision.[10]

The leadership of Agudat Israel rests in the Council of Torah Sages. This is a group of revered rabbies, now seventeen in number. Many are the heads of religious schools and the leaders of autonomous communities. The council operates according to consensus that is attained after long and sometimes heated discussion. Members view themselves and their followers as the present generation of religious communities established generations ago. Thus, one faction of the party traces its roots to the Hasidic movement that swept Eastern European Jewry beginning in the eighteenth century. Its present leader is eighty-five-year-old Rabbi Simcha Bonim Alter (The Gure Rebbe), and its spokesman in the Knesset is Rabbi Abraham Shapira. After many generations, the group remains in conflict with the "opponents" or "Lithuanians," led by eighty-six-year-old Rabbi Eliezer Schach. Their spokesman in the Knesset is Rabbi Shlomo Lorentz. [11]

The prominence of Agudat Israel in the Begin government reflects its reputation of religiosity and its internal discipline. Agudat Israel has also benefited from the narrow margin of the government over the opposition. With the start of the second Begin government in 1981, the prime minister assembled a coalition that included only 61 out of 120 Knesset members. Agudat Israel and the National Religious party accounted for ten places in the government coalition; the ethnoreligious Tami accounted for another three. The threats of Agudat Israel were that it—like other parties—could topple the coalition by its departure and—unlike other parties—could raise religious issues that the NRP and Tami could not afford to oppose without risking their standing among religious voters.

POLITICS OF THE OTHER-WORDLY

The numerous communities that comprise the Agudat Israel complicate the task of political analysis. The divergent positions of community leaders defy generalization. The party press generally does not reveal the nature of internal conflicts. There is precious little published research about the religious parties. One study published in recent years received sharp criticism for its lack of sensitivity to important details of each movement's politics. [12] Even scholars whose credentials make them "religious insiders" have trouble recording the activities of certain communities. For example, one passage in a book published by the religious university Bar Ilan could have been written about an isolated tribe in the deepest part of the jungle. ''Although few details are known about this group, what is known about their religious extremism places them in an intermediate position.''[13]

The leaders of Agudat Israel are rabbis as well as politicians. The bases upon which they define their functions are traditions more than two millenia old, and contemporary political alignments and antagonisms. They await the coming of the Messiah, while seeking to improve conditions for their followers. They speak and write in a style that reveals a pragmatic concern for party patronage in the very near present, as well as a theological concern for everlasting values and a confidence in their own interpretations of those values.

How does one discern when such people are stating a position to which they will adhere with fanaticism, and when they are suggesting the outlines of a bargain? In order to gauge the party's accomplishments, its real desires must be defined. However, some items are entered on the party's shopping list as theatrics in order to impress supporters that Agudat Israel is sufficiently pious, and to wean voters from other religious parties like NRP and Tami. It is in the nature of political theatre that insiders are not candid in ranking priorities. In the context of Israeli religious parties, it is important that unbending orthodoxy be demonstrated. Participants do not concede that financial support of religious schools is more important than the use of religious law to define Who is a Jew. The author began this study of religious parties with the assumption that all religious issues entered into the formal agreement between the parties in the government coalition are equally important. He came to accept the claim of some informants that the issues truly important to Agudat Israel are those which it has pushed to actual implementation.

The Demands of Agudat Israel: Spiritual and Material

Like Israel's secular political parties, Agudat Israel demands certain tangible benefits for its supporters. Unlike the secular parties, it also demands the extention of Jewish religious law into fields where, in the view of the party's leaders, it is not adequately observed. Party leaders often cloak their demands for material benefits in spiritual verbiage. The more clearly *spiritual* demands that Agudat Israel succeeded in writing into the 1981 government coalition agreement are:

1. Strengthening government policy against abortion.
2. Strengthening the protection of Jewish gravesites against the activities of archaeologists, road builders, or property developers.
3. Strengthening policy against autopsies.
4. Facilitating the excuse of women from military services.
5. Strengthening policy forbidding work on the sabbath and religious holidays.
6. Applying of religious law to the state's determination of who is a Jew and insisting that only conversions carried out by orthodox rabbis will be recognized.
7. Opposing the activities of Christian missionaries.
8. Strengthening regulations against the production or sale of nonkosher food.
9. Forbidding swearing in the name of God in court proceedings.

Another group of demands focuses on material issues that Agudat Israel considers requirements for the fulfillment of religious commandments. Those written into the coalition agreement include the provision of separate swimming beaches for men and women; the provision of synagogues and ritual bathes; and the provision of kosher hotels for religious travelers.

Agudat Israel also seeks housing for religious families. It asserts that such housing should be separate from the housing of secular families in order to facilitate collective observances of religious law, freedom from disturbances, such as transportation or sports on Sabbath, and the education of children in a totally religious environment. The pursuit of ample housing is also justified as aiding families who adhere to the biblical requirement of producing numerous children.

Agudat Israel demands state subsidies for its religious institutions, especially schools. A number of informants claim that this is the party's most important demand; it is also the area in which the party has its most tangible record of success. Financial support gains its importance from the character of the party's members. Many male members of the party remain full-time students in a religious school (yeshiva) several years after marriage. Students depend on their yeshiva for free tuition, meals, and a stipend to help support growing families. Some of the party's members remain as yeshiva students all their adult lives. Others work full time as teachers in a yeshiva.

The party also demands that the military excuse all men who study in a yeshiva from service. (A parallel exemption is not granted to students at secular universities.) Agudat Israel justifies this by asserting that religious education is essential for the perpetuation of Jewish values. Party leaders put such values ahead of competing secular interests, like defense of the state. One issue is best described as an item of convenience for observant Jews. Agudat Israel joins the NRP in opposing daylight savings time, which it says will upset the prayer schedules of individuals and synagogues.

The party seeks the inclusion of its poorer neighborhoods and crowded schools into the framework of Project Renewal, a government program to provide physical con-

struction and social programs for distressed urban neighborhoods and small towns. Agudat Israel asserts that
residents of its poor neighborhoods live virtuous, family-
oriented lives in contrast to residents of the problem-ridden
secular neighborhoods included earlier in Project Renewal.
The party further asserts that despite their lack of social
problems, the poor religious neighborhoods can be improved physically. In the eyes of Agudat Israel, these
neighborhoods deserve their share of government largesse.

The party does not make an issue of government jobs
for its members. Cynics note that government-supported
stipends and lack of tuition at religious schools means that
many party members do not work and lack the secular
training demanded of functionaries in a modern state. Agudat Israel makes a point of not asking for ministerial appointments. It wishes to avoid responsibility for what may
be viewed by some of its followers as unacceptable violations of Sabbath rest and other religious provisions. However, the party has demanded a series of senior posts in the
ministries. These are to be party watchdogs to whom religious Jews can address complaints about ministries' activities. The party has also demanded—and obtained—the following strategic posts in the system that distributes public
resources: chairman of the Knesset Finance Committee,
chairman of the government coalition, and a seat on the National Steering Committee of Project Renewal.

Hamodea continuously reminds its readers of how
party representatives press demands upon the government. Many are routine and seem to be made and reported
as much to impress party followers as to change policy.
There are frequent communications with the prime minister, other ministers, and mayors of large cities about alleged
violations of the Sabbath. Often these communications are
provoked by local party committees that spot violations of
religious norms. The newspaper publishes letters from
ministers that order the cessation of nonessential Sabbath

work, or that order inquiries and discipline against employees who violate the Sabbath. *Hamodea* reports meetings between ministers and other secular figures accused of violating religious law and party leaders who admonish them to behave more responsibly. The newspaper reports how party figures presented their demands fully and clearly, while the explanations of secular figures are flawed with respect to their knowledge of the law or the facts at issue.

Agudat Israel as Policy-Maker

Agudat Israel has a mixed record as a policy-maker. On the one hand it has placed numerous demands on the government's agenda and elicited formal agreements that they be enacted. On the other hand, the actual implementation of these provisions has been limited. Perhaps the record of Agudat Israel will improve with time and further experience within the government. Yet, time and experience may not solve the problem of Agudat Israel. The party's problems may be more fundamental. The party cannot achieve many of its goals without adding to the administrative responsibilities of the Chief Rabbinate or other state functionaries. This accommodation represents a continuing conflict for some of its leaders.

The most prominent success of Agudat Israel came at the framing of the coalition agreements between the parties supporting Prime Minister Menachem Begin in 1977 and 1981. Thirty of the eighty-three items listed in the 1981 agreement dealt with religious issues. Many of these were commitments by the new government to carry forward movements that had begun during the 1977 to 1981 period: to prohibit work on the Sabbath and religious holidays; to prohibit the sale of pork and other nonkosher food; to increase the role of religious law in matters of marriage and population registration, including "who is a Jew"; to increase the privileges of religious people in the armed services; and to tighten controls on the work of archaeologists with respect to the preservation of Jewish burial sites. Among the new issues in the 1981 coalition agreement were financial aid to religious schools and other institutions, new housing in religious neighborhoods, the inclusion of religious neighborhoods in Project Renewal, and the appointment of religious persons to senior administrative posts.

In summary, four Agudat Israel members of the Knesset (6 percent of Begin's coalition) were identified with some 36 percent of the items adopted by the 1981 coalition partners. Viewed by secular commentators, the picture was awesome; viewed by Agudat Israel, however, these were only partial successes. Reports in *Hamodea* reveal that members of its communities wanted to achieve goals more clearly religious in nature. Some of these were:

1.   to make the ban on abortions absolute;
2.   to make even more complete the ban on sports, recreation, cultural activities, and commercial activities on the Sabbath (including football,[14] radio and television broadcasts, organized nature walks, and the limited public transportation that is now permitted)[15];
3.   to forbid heart transplants[16];
4.   to forbid military service for all women, even those who would volunteer.[17]

Such demands, when given some legitimacy by their inclusion in the party's press, complicate the task of judging the policy success of Agudat Israel. They suggest that substantial elements in the party aspire to achievements even beyond those accepted by the party in the government's coalition agreement. Perhaps the party's coalition items were minimal positions that various party factions could accept without splintering; or the most they could achieve from their secular partners in the coalition.

The religious items in the coalition agreement differ in the kinds of responses they require. On several points, the agreement commits the government to operate in certain ways. On other points, e.g., the religious communities' share of government financing, there is only a commitment that the government concern itself with the issues at hand. The coalition agreement does not establish explicit monetary targets. The provision for defining who is a Jew according to religious law committed only the prime minister—and not the coalition parties—to support the position of Agudat Israel. For many items, no specification of a deadline for implementation exists.

Agudat Israel has shown flexibility in accepting the formulations of the coalition agreement. It has also shown flexibility around the implementation of its demands. To date, the party has both pushed for and retreated from the religious items in the 1981 agreement.

Achievements of Agudat Israel: Money and Other Tangibles

Agudat Israel has moved to the dining table of the Israeli state. Institutions associated with it stood to receive 12 percent of the government's allotments for education and culture for 1982.[18] Its teacher training colleges for women were excused from program-wide spending cuts ordered by the minister of education and culture.[19] During periods when the government suffered a shortage of cash, religious institutions were authorized to draw on bank loans, whose repayment would be made by the government.[20] Students at religious institutions of higher learning received government financed stipends and were included in the framework of the minimum income law.[21] On several occasions the party press proclaimed allocations of housing blocs set aside for religious families by public or private housing companies.[22] Religious neighborhoods and education institutions associated with Agudat Israel won inclusion in Project Renewal.[23] A summary of the 1982 budget shows that the Ministry of Religions' funds would increase 390 percent in real purchasing power, while the general pattern was budgetary stability or decline in real purchasing power (i.e., taking account of inflation).[24]

The largesse enjoyed by Agudat Israel has brought protests. Secular opponents of the government charge that support for religion came at the expense of needy groups, by a government that was blind to the country's social gap.[25] For their part, the parliamentarians of Agudat Israel asserted overall modesty in their claims on the government treasury. They said that religious schools associated with Agudat Israel received government funding at only 45 percent of the level received by other schools. They also emphasized their communities' self-reliance and their discomfort at too close a relationship with the state. They value their Israeli and international networks of voluntary fundraising, which they want to preserve as important components of their religious communities and fear becoming too dependent on the single resource of state funding, should its control fall into other hands and prove unreliable.[26]

Other protests about the funding of religious institutions have come from the religious sector itself. Wall posters attacking the financial distributions made by Agudat Israel members of the Knesset appeared in religious neighborhoods. Spokesmen from competing religious movements asserted that funds went disproportionately to institutions associated with the parliamentarians' own party factions.[27] Israel's state comptroller also raised his voice against the irregular distribution of resources (aid equivalent to 20 million U.S. dollars for some two hundred institutions[28]) without systematic oversight.

The Army and Religious Recruits

The army is another field where Agudat Israel has scored tangible gains. In pursuit of its theological goal that women should not serve in the army, the party won a change in the procedures used by religious women to claim exemption. In the past, it was necessary for religious women to present themselves before a review committee established by the military, and to convince the committee that they were entitled to exemption because of their beliefs and life styles. Now it is only necessary for women to submit a notarized statement of their religious commitment. Exemptions are automatic; the army is able to investigate *post hoc* and bring charges against women whose life styles are found to be at variance with their declarations. The new procedures went into effect as a result of the 1977 coalition agreement, and there was an immediate increase in the number of women exempted from military service—from 21 percent of the age cohort in 1976, to 27 percent in 1977, and 32 percent in 1978. There were several protests against these new procedures. University students claimed they would impose a greater burden of national defense on secular persons.[29] However, Agudat Israel won additional commitments as a result of the 1981 coalition agreement. The defense minister declared that the military would continue or increase concessions to students and teachers at religious institutions seeking exemptions from duty, and would arrange religious lectures at military bases.[30]

El Al: Israel Airlines

Once out of the realms of money and the military, the record of Agudat Israel is more problematic. In the case of the party's demand of El Al—that it cease all flights on the Sabbath—it ran into the intense opposition of the company's workers. Moreover, the company's records of financial health and employee morale were not up to the pressures. At stake was perhaps an additional $40 million (U.S. dollars) of annual losses for the company and individual losses for employees whose jobs depended on Sabbath flights or who received bonus pay for Sabbath work. The company had suffered more than sixty strikes and other work stoppages in the ten years preceding 1982 and its 1982 losses were $234 million.[31]

Agudat Israel won an explicit mention of El Al's Sabbath flights in the 1981 coalition agreement, and subsequently pushed the issue with greater intensity than demands it pursued for cessation of other Sabbath work. The national airline violated the Sabbath with more national and international prominence than other government companies. Its flights were not justified on the grounds of health or national defense. Unlike steel mills or concrete plants, the company could not claim that operations had to continue for technical reasons seven days a week.

In response to those who claimed that Agudat Israel was threatening the principle of the status quo, the party claimed that El Al's Sabbath flights were themselves a violation of the status quo. They pointed out that the flights had been initiated as special accommodations for Christian pilgrims, and had evolved into regular flights for anyone willing to buy a ticket. Party leaders mocked El Al for not including the Sabbath flights on the regular timetable, thus preserving the fiction that they were only special events. Agudat Israel also noted that there were no Sabbath flights to and from the United States, in order to avoid offending the large number of religious American Jews.

At the beginning of Begin's second term, the Council of Torah Sages gave the government six months to comply with the coalition agreement to end Sabbath flights. When that deadline passed, the council complained that the prime minister had given his personal commitment to implement the El Al clause. The council planned to meet every two months in order to oversee progress. The government appointed a committee to investigate the financial and technical implications of stopping Sabbath flights. In response, Knesset members of Agudat Israel asserted that financial loss was not an appropriate reason for violating the Sabbath. They recalled the commitment of all coalition members to cease the flights and offered to raise contributions from religious Jews in order to finance the Sabbath closing.[32] The transportation minister promised that the flights would cease no matter what the conclusions of the committee, but nontheless asked that the committee be allowed to continue its deliberations.[33]

Liberal party members of the government coalition indicated their opposition to implementing the El Al section of the coalition agreement. In response to threats from Agudat Israel to withdraw from the coalition if the agreement was not honored, the liberals made the same threat if the agreement was honored.

The opposition of El Al workers was strong. At one point they enforced a blockade at the entrance to Israel's international airport, and harassed all religious Jews who were dressed in the Hasidic style of wide-brimmed black hats and long black coats. Israeli television carried pictures of angry families who, kept from their flights, loudly recalled the pogroms of Europe. In the fall of 1982, the workers won a temporary court order preventing the government from stopping Sabbath flights. While that order had yet to run its course, the whole issue of Sabbath flights was lost in the greater chaos of El Al. Stewardesses struck against the company rule requiring them to sell duty-free items during flights, and the company responded with a general lockout. Company directors presented a list of demands to the workers, including the acceptance of several hundred dismissals as an economy move. The airline remained closed for several months; it reopened without Sabbath flights. In the meantime, however, other Israeli airlines—Maof and Arkia—expanded their operations on the Sabbath and hired some of El Al's personnel. Agudat Israel has refrained from pressing the demand made by some of its supporters that the Airport Authority cease all commercial flights on the Sabbath.[34]

Abortion

Agudat Israel was able to change formal procedures for obtaining an abortion. There is some question about its success in changing actual practice. During the 1977 to 1981 period, Agudat Israel succeeded in changing the abortion law. Despite harsh public opposition, no longer would "sociological considerations" be among the criteria that health care professionals could use to justify abortions in public hospitals. However, "psychological considerations" have remained among the legal criteria. According to some reports, "psychological considerations" are now being used to justify requests that previously would have been approved under sociological criteria. Moreover, the change in the law has not kept physicians from performing abortions in private clinics.

Agudat Israel sought to deal with the problem of implementation by the appointment of a senior advisor in the Health Ministry. His mission was to sit on various ministerial panels that deal with abortion, and work towards the gradual elimination of all abortions.[35] The advisor became known for his outspoken opinions. He compared abortions to Nazi genocide, and declared that they deprive the Israeli Army of important manpower. In response, secular critics reminded the country that Agudat Israel itself deprives the Army of manpower via the exemptions received by students in its religious institutions. In November 1982—less than five months after the advisor's appointment—the Health Ministry declared that the advisor would not define the ministry's policy on abortion, nor would he sit on committees that deal with individual requests.[36]

Who Is a Jew?

This issue of theological importance has nagged religious and secular parties since the creation of modern Israel. According to Jewish Law, a Jew is a person born to a Jewish mother or converted to Judaism after instruction and examination by a recognized rabbi. Which rabbis are recognized is one element of the dispute. In Israel only orthodox rabbis have legal standing, and they refuse to accept conversions performed outside of Israel by rabbis in the conservative or reform movements. From the orthodox perspective, these movements compromise many essential features of Judaism, and represent a step along the way to assimilation into the Gentile world. Conversions performed by nonorthodox rabbis, according to the orthodox, are often superficial ceremonies to accommodate a person wishing to marry a Jew and not the result of prolonged instruction and intense commitment to Judaism.

Another aspect of the definitional question involves various legal provisions in Israel that apply to Jews. Prominent among these is the Law of Return, which provides entry and eventual citizenship to Jews. Some years ago secular and religious politicians struck a compromise on this issue: non-Jewish spouses and other close relatives would be allowed to benefit from the Law of Return, even if they were not recognized according to religious law as Jews. As part of the 1981 coalition agreement, Agudat Israel won from the prime minister (but not from the entire coalition) an agreement to work toward altering the Law of Return so that it would specify converts according to religious law.

The issue of who is a Jew is one that typifies the constraints on Agudat Israel. Many of its own members, and communities even further to the right on the religious spectrum press for the application of religious law. When such an issue is raised, Agudat Israel is forced to respond positively by supporting the definition of who is a Jew according to religious law. Its leaders cannot allow themselves to be cited for compromising basic issues of religious law.

Even raising the question of who is a Jew generates sharp opposition, both within and outside of Israel. Jews in the conservative and reform movements resent the exclusion of their rabbis from organized Judaism in Israel. For people married to spouses converted by conservative or re-

form rabbis, the issue represents a threat to the Jewish identity of their spouses and children. Secular Jews in Israel also
see the issue in terms of the domino theory: if Agudat Israel
can change the status quo on this issue, a series of other
religious-secular accommodations will ensue. Among
these is the state's policy of recognizing secular marriages
and divorces that are performed outside of Israel.

Agudat Israel has a problem with this issue. Sharp
conflict with secular Jews is something that party leaders
prefer to avoid. If the party gains a point at the expense of
severely alienating secular interests, it may lose that point
and many others when political alignments change. Also,
expanding the role of Jewish law in public matters raises the
issue of who would interpret and enforce individual cases?
Such responsibilities are likely to fall on the Chief Rabbinate and Ministry of Religions, both staffed by supporters of
the National Religious party. In the eyes of some Agudat
Israel leaders, it is better to sacrifice an issue than to augment the role of the NRP in religious issues.[37]

Agudat Israel has behaved ambivalently toward the
matter of who is a Jew. It has alternately pushed the issue
and withdrawn in the face of hesitancy from its own leaders
or a realization that it lacked the requisite votes in the Knesset.[38] While some party leaders express reservations, others
press the issue. According to informants within and outside the religious communities, more than a little theatrics
surround the subject. Once the determination that certain
rabbis wish to avoid pressing the issue is made, the matter
becomes an obvious topic for their rivals to promote. Thus
the reluctant are embarrassed for insufficient orthodoxy.[39]

Prime Minister Begin also wavered on the issue. In the
spring of 1982 Begin signaled his support for Knesset consideration of who is a Jew seemingly as part of a package
that included his support for Agudat Israel's position on El
Al Sabbath flights, in exchange for the party's support
when he ordered religious as well as secular settlers re-

moved from northern Sinai.[40] Some months later, however, the prime minister was more attuned to the outcry from conservative and reform Jews in the Diaspora, at which time he asked Agudat Israel's leadership not to raise the definitional question for a while.[41] The prime minister supported the introduction of the issue to the Knesset in March 1983. The issue did not attract the full support of coalition parties, and was dropped from the Knesset's agenda. Agudat Israel did not threaten to abandon the coalition at that time. Perhaps is it significant that in the same week the Finance Ministry approved a budget supplement for the support of Yeshiva students with large families.

Archaeology

Here again, Agudat Israel clashes with right-wingers and secularists. The issue at hand is archaeological digs that threaten ancient Jewish grave sites. Proper care of and respect for the dead is sacred to religious Jews. Moreover, the disturbance of Jewish grave sites recalls desecrations by European and Arab vandals. Israeli archaeologists are willing to respect Jewish graves, but they want professional, scientific determination of the sites. Agudat Israel, on the other hand, prefers that the Chief Rabbinate and the Ministry of Religions issue archaeological permits. Archeologists want this power to remain with the Antiquities Department of the Ministry of Education and Culture.

In defending their profession, archeologists cite their contributions to the Zionist revival. Archeological findings point to the rich strata of ancient Jewish civilization in Israel, and thus lend credence to Zionist claims of Jewish roots in the Holy Land. In support of their position, archeologists cite the support of the late Rabbi Abraham Yitzhak Hacohen Kook, a prominent figure in the development of the National Religious party. The influential academic community supports the archeologists, as part of a general posture that science should not be obstructed by religious interference.[42]

Agudat Israel has lost few opportunities to remind the religious community that the National Religious party controls the Ministry of Education and Culture and that the NRP's minister has supported the archaeologists. During 1981 and 1982, numerous confrontations between religious Jews, archaeologists, and the police took place at a contested site close to the old city of Jerusalem. *Hamodea* attacked the minister of education and culture for failing to recognize the Jewish graves there. Archaeologists, in their turn, asserted that the bones displayed by religious Jews had come from chickens of dubious antiquity. When physical conflict between religious Jews and the police occurred, Agudat Israel accused the minister in charge of the police—also a member of the National Religious party—of brutality.[43]

Agudat Israel seems to have withdrawn from the archaeological issue without having seen the implementation of the coalition agreement. The power of the academic community combined with those segments of the National Religious party in control of the Ministry of Education and Culture was too strong. On a related issue, however, Agudat Israel was successful. With the support of the prime minister, it achieved the removal of bones and other human remnants from the laboratories of archaeologists (where they had been taken for study) and their return to proper graves.[44]

Religious politics in Israel is a pot pourri of several parties and numerous factions. Competition between religious organizations with different theological and political outlooks is at least as great as competition between religious and secular parties. Agudat Israel is currently prominent in the religious sector; of the parties in the Knesset and the government coalition, it is the most stridently religious. However, its leadership is hampered by struggles with its own right wing and even more extreme religious factions, and its ambivalence toward the state and the National Religious party. Agudat Israel is not comfortable with the Chief Rabbinate and the Ministry of Religions. While the party cannot resist prodding from the right to advance the values of traditional Judaism, it cannot accept the demands of right-wingers on issues like who is a Jew without adding to the power of suspect bodies associated with the state.

Agudat Israel has a mixed record with respect to implementing its goals. The party's clearest successes came in having many points written into the 1981 coalition agreement, and filling the strategic posts of chairman in the government coalition, chairman of the Knesset Finance Committee, and membership on the national steering committee of Project Renewal. It has also done well in gaining material support for religious institutions, housing for religious families, and easier procedures for religious girls to avoid military service. Agudat Israel can obtain material satisfaction for itself without directly challenging competing interests. To be sure, some secular politicians claim that increased support for religious institutions comes at the expense of their own favorite programs. In a sharply inflationary setting, however, with the budget changing several times each year, it is difficult to designate real winners and losers. Where competing interests are challenged directly by its demands, Agudat Israel has done less well. It won a victory in the case of El Al Sabbath flights, against the sharp opposition of airline employees. However, other Israeli airlines have taken up the slack in the foregone flights and have hired some of El Al's personnel. Issues like who is a Jew, forbidding abortions, and putting the control of archaeologists directly in the hands of rabbis threaten established interests that are powerful in Israeli society. Under such conditions, Agudat Israel has not been able to rely on the leaders of political parties who signed a detailed coalition agreement in 1981. Neither, with respect to these issues, has Agudat Israel been able to rely on itself. The party has proven reluctant to fight intense secular opponents to final resolutions and has wavered in the face of bestowing significant new religious authority on state functionaries.

CHAPTER 5

Budgeting Amidst Triple-Digit Inflation

GOVERNMENT BUDGETS PLAY A KEY ROLE IN THE activities of policy-makers; they also attract a great deal of attention from political scientists. Perhaps no other aspect of policy-making is so completely described and analyzed.[1] For both policy-makers and political scientists, the budget is the ultimate scoreboard, showing which agencies, programs, or groups are getting more or less of what the government has to offer. The professional thinking and sophisticated research about budgeting has focused on conditions when prices have been stable. If money is the lifeblood of government, the budget is its heart.

But what happens when currency loses its power to predict the value of goods? One study of budgeting in poor countries describes conditions of high inflation.[2] Budgeting loses its annual character, as a once-a-year event. The central budget office and spending departments struggle constantly to direct the flow of slippery and ill-defined resources. Participants invent tricks and counter-tricks to protect their share of the pie. The central collection and publication of data suffers greatly. Spending departments try to satisfy contractors with vouchers that may wait for months—untallied—before they are honored by the Treasury. Spenders also do what they can to establish autonomous accounts—free from Treasury control. The Treasury, for its part, hides what information it possesses in order not to reveal how much it can actually allocate to hungry departments. There is a difference between the official, published budget, and the "real budget" that is said to be in the notebooks or minds of an inner elite. The true rate of inflation, as well as the true allocation of resources, may be hidden in a system of poor data collection and purposeful efforts to be misleading. In many poor countries the obscure character of inflationary budgeting results partly from the closed character of politics and the weakness of the government technocracy.

Israel, however, with her competitive democratic regime and sophisticated bureaucracy, has long been among the world leaders in inflation. Israel's consumer price index (CPI) increased by an average of 9 percent annually in the period from 1968 to 1973; it increased to an annual rate of 36 percent from 1974 to 1977; 51 percent in 1978; 78 percent in 1979; 131 percent in 1980; 117 percent in 1981; and 131 percent in 1982.[3]

The Israeli government budget has moved upward at a pace no less impressive than the consumer price index. Records are tardy, because supplemental budgets are enacted retroactively to cover commitments made earlier. Total figures compiled by the state comptroller were 21.9 billion shekels for 1978, 45.2 billion for 1979, and 105.7 billion for 1980.[4] The concept of a truly annual budget has disappeared. In each recent year, one or two major supplemental budgets together have amounted to some 47 percent of the budget as originally authorized.

Under the pressures of inflation, the Knesset has

eased the procedures for budget changes. In order to arrange a greater line of credit from the Bank of Israel, the Finance Ministry need only obtain the agreement of the Knesset Finance Committee. On his own authority, having only to inform the Knesset Finance Committee of his actions, the finance minister can allocate to each program a sum up to 15 percent of its authorized spending from the "General Reserve," an item amounting to 3.4 percent of the total budget for 1982.

THE CHARACTER OF ISRAELI INFLATION

Israeli inflation is hedged by the extensive use of price indexation to link incomes and payments to increasing prices. The value of the shekel with respect to foreign currencies drops continuously, so the costs in shekels of imports and foreign travel increase.[5] The gross national product (GNP) has increased at a rate close to that of the government budget.[6] Personal incomes have risen along with the cost-of-living index.[7] There is not a perfect correspondence between the various indicators. At least temporarily, some groups lose while others gain in purchasing power. In general, however, goods and services tend to cost about the same, in real terms, from one period to another.

In such a setting, one set of price increases triggers another, along with increases in incomes and the amount of shekels that must be paid to foreign creditors. Public consciences like the state comptroller and the Bank of Israel assert that inflation is bad. In policy-making circles, however, contrary pressures exist. For many, the problems of inflation are not so bad that their own favored programs should be cut back. During the Begin government, the general strategy was to cope, rather than to battle all out against inflation.

Critics of the government feared that a crisis was on the way. They asserted that the machinery of linkages and stable real purchasing power depended on outside resources, thus increasing Israel's balance of payments deficit and foreign debt during the period of triple-digit inflation.[8]

Budgeting from the Perspective of the Finance Ministry

In Israel, as in other parliamentary democracies, the Finance Ministry is guardian of the treasury against the spending requests of other ministries.[9] The Budget Department of the Finance Ministry receives program requests from the ministries and formulates budget statements for Knesset review and approval. Another unit of the Finance Ministry—the Accountant General—implements the budget via periodic allotments of funds to the ministries. In many countries, the allotment step is routine, providing something close to 25 percent of a unit's budget every three months. In Israel, however, the profile of the Accountant General increased during the period of triple-digit inflation to that of an important gatekeeper regulating the flow of spending.

As in other countries, Israeli budget categories exert practical control on only a small percentage of annual spending. Most expenditures are, in practical terms, virtually unadjustable: the amount for civil servants' salaries moves upward in response to automatic cost-of-living adjustments and periodic boosts that are highly political in nature; sums for educational programs, housing, health, and other services are allowed to keep pace with the numbers of people who present demands and meet program qualifications; established formulas obligate the government to support a major portion of municipal expenditures; debt service (33 percent of the 1982 budget) and other legal obligations are considered untouchable. What is left for control by budget makers and the Accountant General is the level of adjustable program activity. These are the activities that can be postponed or stopped without violating firm commitments. This is estimated as somewhere between 10 and 20 percent of total spending. Even the latter is affected by the reluctance of Israeli budgeteers. Like their counterparts elsewhere, Israelis do not want to reduce the established bases of program service levels.

The literature on budgeting in poor countries describes a collapse of orderly financial planning and allocation under conditions of high inflation. Although Israel's budget process shows numerous strains and adjustments, there has not been such a collapse. Comprehensive indexing automates many of the adjustments that elsewhere would trouble budget makers. Economists and other budgeting professionals express their frustration at not being able to plan according to rational models, but their complaints are not too different from counterparts in Western countries with stable currencies. It has been a long while since political scientists expected truly rational planning or allocation in government budget categories.[10]

STRATEGIES

Two strategies are apparent in the Finance Ministry's budget practices of recent years. One has been to routinize a number of functions that previously required specific decisions from high-level officials. Another has been to increase the power of central officials in the ministry by improving their information about the spending ministries and by increasing their control over key points in the budget process. Both strategies work to tighten the Finance Ministry's control over government management.

Under the heading of routinization, the Finance Ministry has increased the fine tuning of the linkage mechanisms that tie a number of outlays to inflation. In the process, the ministry has saved the time of its own senior officials and those in spending units who previously had to reach agreement on many specific authorizations for spending adjustments.[11] Major examples appear in the sector of municipal finance, where the taxes and fees collected by local authorities are now effectively pegged to the consumer price index. Earlier, local government revenues had lagged behind inflation and left municipalities short of the resources needed to support their services. No longer is it necessary to mount a campaign in order to increase this kind of local government income or to cope with the opposition of politicians who proclaim that taxes and service charges are already too high.

The Finance Ministry and the Central Bureau of Statistics have developed several inflation indexes besides the general CPI that help settle arguments about the unsuitability of the CPI in certain programs. There are specialized indexes for the wholesale prices of industrial outputs, housing construction, road paving, and agricultural inputs. Work is continuing to develop other indexes, including those for imports of military hardware and health services.

Along with its efforts to routinize or simplify certain procedures, the Finance Ministry has also sought to improve its information. Since the advent of high inflation, the Finance Ministry has added several items to its routine flow of budget information, and has improved the quality of information that flowed earlier. Annual budget statements now report the amount of contractual authority to be allowed each ministry and other government units. Earlier, the ministries and other bodies had exploited a weakness in the Finance Ministry's control network by contracting for the future delivery (and payment) of goods and services;

thus, they avoided budget controls that had been imposed on current spending alone.

Currently, there is a more accurate reporting of personnel employed by local authorities as well as by government ministries. Now the Finance Ministry can more readily enforce personnel ceilings via one of its component units, the Civil Service Commission. Personnel controls have also been strengthened with respect to the large number of government-owned companies. Increases in salaries and other benefits are now limited by the increases granted to regular government employees. The salaries of senior company employees are pegged to those at comparable levels in the ministries. In charge of supervising this strategy is yet another unit of the Finance Ministry—the Authority for Government Companies.

The Finance Ministry has substantially increased the profile of its accountant general's department. A new unit in that department prepares monthly reports of cash flows and spending projections. Its reports feed into the decision of senior staff with respect to the allotments that will be released to each ministry for the coming period. The Finance Ministry has also put greater emphasis on a long-standing formal power of the accountant general—the review and approval of terms for loan programs (e.g., housing)—that will obligate the treasury into the future.

The most prominent current role of the accountant general is entitled "budgeting via the cash window." The Finance Ministry has taken the largely routine task of periodically releasing a portion of each year's budget allotment and turned this practice into a mechanism to restrain spending. The purposes are to keep each allotment as small as possible, to postpone spending (and thus to minimize the real value of each shekel spent), to oppose the tendency of ministries to spend quickly, and to minimize developments of new programs or expansions of existing ones.

The accountant general relies on a central staff of referents (each of whom deals with the periodic allotments of funds to one or several ministries), plus other staff members who are seconded as resident accountants in each spending ministry. Each month the resident accountant filters initial requests from the ministry for the coming allotment, and the central office referent generally seeks to reduce the allotment even further. The accountant general's technocrats in the ministries and the central office seek to reach accords that will satisfy their masters at the policy levels. Unresolved cases reach forums that also involve—in ascending order of importance—the director general of the Spending Ministry and the accountant general himself, the director general of the Finance Ministry, the ministers of finance and the Spending Ministry, and ultimately, the prime minister.[12] In the recent period of high inflation, the accountant general has, in practice, acquired some of the work previously done by the Budget Department of the Finance Ministry. As a result, the bureaucratic prestige of the accountant general's department has increased, while that of the Budget Department has declined.

The pressures of the Finance Ministry on the other ministries begin early in the budget process, when the Finance Ministry announces the inflation forecast to be used in formulating each ministry's budget for the coming year. At this stage the Finance Ministry has, in recent years, taken two steps designed to reduce spending. First, its choice of an inflation prediction comes from the low side of the range forecast by its economists. (Some maintain that its forecast is intentionally *below* the range actually foreseen). Second, it cuts the announced forecast further by insisting that a certain percentage of the increase in spending be held by the Finance Ministry as a government-wide reserve. For the 1982 budget Finance Ministry informants report that initial estimates for the year's inflation were in the range of 110 to 120 percent. The official forecast was 100 percent, with a reserve of 10 percent to be withheld from initial program allocations. Thus, the spending increase initially granted ranged 90 percent above that of the previous budget.

The Finance Ministry has also worked with the Interior Ministry and the Bank of Israel to close one avenue used by municipalities to evade national budget controls. Local authorities had lines of credit with commercial banks, and occasionally borrowed foreign currency from non-Israeli banks. The banks cooperated on the assumption that the central government would bail out the local authorities rather than allow them to default. The Finance Ministry has sought to regulate and minimize this channel of local finance. It has set annual limits on bank borrowing by local authorities, and requires explicit authorizations for each loan made by the Interior Ministry. The Finance Ministry deals directly with the banks through regulations issued by the Bank of Israel.

Several actions taken by the Finance Ministry have generated dispute and rancor. A number of senior technocrats feel that they have lost status in the face of excessive centralization and reliance on shortsighted pragmatic judgments. Some of them have advocated the abandonment of a shekel-based budget for one based on U.S. dollars or on another currency. They explain their defeat by the realities of politics. It is difficult for the Finance Minister to defend a budget known to be final and unchangeable against the demands of spending ministries and their client allies. It is easier to enact a budget in shekels that will require a great deal of reworking during the year (i.e., one or two major supplements and twelve monthly allotments). During the year, the Finance Minister can hold back additional allocations that are not so much in the public eye. Some of the technocrats opposed to the minister's strategy concede his wisdom, even while they balk at the subordinate and artificial roles they are required to play. The finance minister himself seemed finally to have accepted the view of those advocating "dollarization." During the first days of the

Shamir government, Finance Minister Yoram Aridor proposed to link the entire Israeli economy to the U.S. dollar; he resigned when his fellow ministers rejected the idea.

The Spending Ministries

Israel's Finance Ministry may be the most dominant actor in the budget process, but it is not alone. It must contend with some seventeen ministries and numerous other spending units like municipalities and government-owned companies. The spenders have developed a series of behaviors that are suitable to high inflation. Informal ''dollarization'' is one example. Government regulations and national pride require that most official budget documents be submitted in shekels. Formal exceptions include components of the Defense Ministry's budget, and the budgets of certain other units that make extensive purchases abroad. These budgets are denominated in U.S. dollars. Informally, many units also plan in U.S. dollars. They calculate the number of work units or projects they want to perform and estimate total costs in dollars. Only at the last minute, when required to present their estimates, do they translate the dollar amounts into shekels.

Several tricks are designed to maximize each ministry's position in the budget competition. Some of these resemble those described by Aaron Wildavsky in 1964.[13] These may be all the more attractive under the pressures of inflation. The budget officer of one ministry cited Wildavsky as she reported how she presents information to the Finance Ministry's Budget Department and Accountant General. Some of the ''tricks'' follow.

Pad. One of the oldest of budget tricks is to ask for more than is really needed. This is made no less attractive by inflation that is likely to be higher than the figure officially forecast by the Finance Ministry.

Spend early.   With the value of currency declining at a rate that may exceed 10 percent per month, the prize goes to the unit that spends the fastest, thereby maximizing the value of goods and services received for each unit of currency.

Anticipate cuts from official budget commitments, and spend even more quickly than usual.   The Finance Ministry is likely to impose special restraints on spending in response to unexpected upward thrusts in prices or other unforeseen events. For example, soon after military action began in Lebanon during June 1982, some ministries increased pressures on their operating officers to finalize agreements with contractors.

Contract.   In the early period of high inflation, contracting was a widely used method of evading the Finance Ministry's spending controls. Because the future outlays associated with contracts did not show up in the current budget (and there was no systematic review of contracts by the Finance Ministry) contracting was a device used to carry on operations outside the budget framework. The bills would come to the Finance Ministry in a later year as legal obligations that must be honored. Now the shekel amounts of contractual authority appear routinely as part of each ministry's budget allocation. Even though the appeal of contracting has been trimmed by this reform, contracting has not lost all of its appeal. It remains attractive as a device to counter the Finance Ministry's efforts to tighten its controls over the hiring of additional personnel. By contracting for certain activities, a ministry can add to its programs without adding to its workforce.

Promise to lease.   Leasing is a variant of contracting. While the Finance Ministry's controls over formal contracting may prevent outright leasing in the current year, a minister or director general may carry enough credibility with a firm to persuade it to begin work on a venture on the basis of an unofficial commitment to use it for an extended period (and thereby affect a future budget only via annual payments).

Delay reporting income from service charges.   The charges and fees that ministries collect from the public are figured into their annual budget allocation. A ministry can use this income to make purchases as soon as it is received and delay reporting it as income to the Finance Ministry until the end of the month, quarter, or, ideally, the year. In the nature of high inflation, income has a higher value when spent by a ministry than when posted against the spending authorized to a ministry on the books of the Finance Ministry.

Delay payment to the Treasury of the income taxes withheld from employees' salaries.   This can amount to a substantial saving for labor-intensive social service agencies in the context of high rates of income taxation.[14] It is a ploy that the Finance Ministry will sometimes accept from municipal authorities and government companies, all the while crediting the workers involved with having paid the taxes withheld from them. The result is an unbudgeted subsidy for the spending units.

Complain when the general consumer price index does not advance quickly enough to cover price increases. Do not complain when the CPI advances more rapidly than prices.   The consumer price index does not accurately measure the price increases actually encountered by each government unit. For some, the CPI goes up more than the price increases of the products they must buy. As a result, their budget increases more than is necessary to support current programs, and they can squirrel away some money to pay for program expansions that are not likely to be approved by the finance ministry.

Technocrats in the Finance Ministry know that the budget and inflation are pulled upward by the system whereby some ministries are satisfied by budget adjustments based on the general CPI, while others demonstrate that the character of their programs require additional boosts beyond those provided by the CPI.[15] Lacking sophisticated indexes suitable to each ministry, the Finance Ministry is powerless to close this particular leak in the dike.

Reduce the quality of goods and services purchased by the ministry, and provided to the public. This tactic has appeal when the Finance Ministry will not formally authorize new programs, and increased allocations are barely sufficient to meet the growing costs of current programs. One of the earliest actions taken by ministries seeking to save something for program development is to cut down on maintenance.[16] Other actions that come under the rubric of reducing quality include increasing the workloads of existing staff; purchasing supplies of lower price and quality; and reducing the hours when services are provided in field offices.

Cut programs that are popular with the public. Municipalities have generated crises by stopping garbage collection, or shutting off the lights at national tourist attractions. Government hospitals have reduced the number of beds or closed entire departments. The uproar caused by laid off workers, strikes begun by their colleagues, or the complaints of citizens has forced the Finance Ministry to authorize additional funds.

Borrow outside the government framework. The Finance Ministry itself went this route in the 1981 election year. It sought an infusion of foreign bank loans rather than advances from the Bank of Israel, and thereby minimized the appearance of deficits in current accounts. Until the Finance Ministry and the Interior Ministry clamped down, municipalities regularly went to Israeli banks for short-term loans, and occasionally borrowed overseas. Even now, when this route is formally under tight control by national ministries and the Bank of Israel, municipal budget officers admit to special deals with commercial banks. They claim that the sums involved are small and for short terms; nonetheless, such deals are departures from the formal rules.

Seek donors. Numerous public institutions that rely on the government budget for much of their resources, such as hospitals and universities, also collect voluntary donations from Israelis and foreigners. The mayor of Jerusalem has established a foundation that raises an amount equivalent to 16 percent of the municipality's budget. Even the military—which commands a third of the government budget—supplements this with donations from patriotic Israelis.

Use the confusion of inflation to request additional funding that will flow to new or expanded programs. The Finance Ministry recognizes that some ministries or municipalities face increased costs that are not met by averaged, system-wide adjustments for inflation. Some tricks are widely recognized but ignored, like the late reporting of a ministry's income from service charges. Spending units also enjoy flexibility with respect to the transfer of funds from one budget item to another. They know that the Finance Ministry cannot look in depth at all of their presentations. Occasionally a budget analyst will spot a wild claim and the analyst will report it in bureaucratic circles or leak it to the press, in order to punish the greedy with public ridicule. However, the spenders' claims of supplements demanded by inflation are assumed to hide some money for new or expanded activities.

Reach agreement with the Finance Ministry that the budget will support a given level of services, no matter what the financial cost. Numerous sources from the Finance Ministry and the spending units report that the budget process has informally evolved to one based largely on the accomplishments of program units, rather than authority to spend money. Thus, the staffs of the Finance Ministry's Budget Department and the accountant general think in terms of the funds needed to maintain current programs in the ministries that they review. Budget personnel in the spending ministries report that their best arguments with the Finance Ministry rest on demonstrations that program clients have increased in number, that costs of specific program-related supplies have grown faster than the CPI, or that equipment that is vital to current programs must be replaced.

Counter-Tactics of the Finance Ministry

Budgeting is competitive; each tactic used by a spending department generates counter-tactics by the Finance Ministry. Technocrats in the Finance Ministry are aware of techniques used by spending departments, although they do not claim to recognize each incident of a spender's tactics at work. The Finance Ministry continues to press the spending ministries. Among its tactics are:

Delay outlays until later in the fiscal year. This is a direct counter to the efforts of other ministries to spend early. Spending that is delayed in the midst of high inflation saves real value for the Finance Ministry at the spender's expense.

Pressure the spending ministries with freezes, cuts, and estimates of near-term inflation that are purposefully low. The point here is to force ministries to prove the case for increases in spending.

Identify spending that is needed to support the continuation of established programs, and that which will be used to expand or improve a ministry's programs. In many cases this simple tactic is made practical by the small size of Israel, and by the experience of budget examiners, the central office referents of the Accountant General, and the employees of the Accountant General who are seconded to the spending ministries.

Punish spending ministries that make poorly documented claims by delaying response to their requests.   A delayed response is a signal of dissatisfaction and carries a cost that increases automatically with inflation. Even if a delayed response ultimately turns into an approval, each week of delay will cost the recipient a reduction in the purchasing power of the funds that are granted.

Generate an atmosphere of restraint.   Budget examiners and the gatekeepers of the accountant general's department recognize that many of their specific decisions invite counter tactics on the part of spending ministries. They do not claim that their efforts result in measurable savings. However, they feel that they contribute to the policy of restraint against inflation. They do not make it easy for spending ministries to obtain resources in excess of those required to keep programs at their current levels. Presentations to units of the Finance Ministry take time that might be used for other purposes. Delegations of senior staff and/ or a minister may be no more successful than the pleas of working level bureaucrats. Spending monitors in various units of the Finance Ministry feel that the weight of procedures keep spending units from being casual in their requests, and lead to a self-selection of the cases that warrant special treatment.

Variations among Spending Units

The Israeli bureaucracy reflects the varied landscape of national politics. Ministries, municipalities, and government companies have unequal weights, and different styles of behavior.

A simple division of the Israeli bureaucracy separates the Ministry of Defense into one category, and everything else into another. Defense regularly takes about one-third of the national government's budget; the army occupies an honored place among the country's institutions, and the financial burdens of defense do not generate protests equivalent to those elsewhere.

The defense budget receives special treatment. It is not subject to the detailed controls of the Accountant General. Instead, the Defense Ministry itself controls the allotment of its annual budget, thereby protecting the defense budget from one of the major tools used by the Finance Ministry to restrain or cut back midyear spending in other ministries. Also, a substantial part of the defense budget is denominated in U.S. dollars. This amount (42 percent of the defense budget initially approved for 1982; 50 percent of the budget for 1981) pays for the import of military supplies and equipment. Because it is denominated in dollars, the sum will not erode with Israeli inflation. Thus, another budget-restraining tool of the Finance Ministry—the low official projection of anticipated inflation—is curtailed in the case of defense. Finally, the Defense Ministry uses some of its vast resources to support sophisticated staff work that feeds into the budget process. More than other ministries, defense can justify its requests in terms of planned exercises and the development of new equipment and facilities. This documentation helps both at the beginning and in the middle of each budget year, when the goal is to head off a retrenchment-minded Finance Ministry.

Other spending units have devised additional budget games. Some of these may be transient in that they depend on the personalities that occupy the positions of minister or director general. Minister of Education Zebulon Hammer, for example, has an esteemed reputation among bureaucratic participants and observers. He is said to be selective in the appeals he, personally, makes to the Finance Ministry. Typically, these appeals are well documented, and the minister is persistent in presenting his case. As a result of

one battle that he waged and lost with the education minister, Begin's second finance minister resigned in January
1981.[17] "If only we had someone like [Education Minister]
Hammer," reported a budget officer in another ministry.
"[Our minister] is too much of a compromiser. He doesn't
push hard enough. In contrast, to our additional sorrow, is
[the director general]. He fights too hard for everything. He
is not selective, and the Finance Ministry does not view his
presentations as credible."

The Interior Ministry plays an important role as a bro-
ker in the budget process. On the one hand, it approaches
the Finance Ministry like every other spender, in the pursuit of money and the freedom to spend it. On the other
hand, it serves as a principal monitor of local authorities,
with the power of approval or veto over budget planning
and implementation. Interior Ministry personnel claim that
they pursue the best deal they can for the local authorities
from the Finance Ministry. They also claim to have increased controls over local authorities that seek to evade
their policies.

In its role as a protector of local authorities, the Interior
Ministry has resisted Finance Ministry directives that do
not have the backing of the government. If such a directive
does not specifically mention local authorities, the Interior
Ministry has assumed that it does not apply to them. It may
be only a matter of time before the Finance Ministry reacts
and sends another directive, more explicit and with the
backing of a government decision. However, even a few
days of extra time can warn alert authorities that something
unpleasant is likely to happen, and lead them to finalize
contracting or hiring procedures. The Interior Ministry has
also tried to soften the Finance Ministry's policy of project-
ing a low estimate of inflation for the budget year, and then
withholding a portion of even that projected increase as an
unprogrammed reserve. The Interior Ministry advises local
authorities to program for the use of the reserve, but not to
release those funds until approval is secured. In the world

of bureaucratic pressures and restraints, this presents the Finance Ministry with an *almost fait accompli*, which may keep it from taking the local authorities' reserves for other uses. Furthermore, the Interior Ministry has sought to provide timely disbursement of its general grant to municipal authorities. Some municipalities invest part of these grants in savings instruments that are linked to the cost of living, and thereby protect some of their budget from midyear inflation erosion.

The Interior Ministry is not entirely supportive of local authorities. It has adhered to the general trends of the Finance Ministry to tighten its own controls on local spending. It has worked with the Finance Ministry and the Bank of Israel to restrict bank borrowing as an alternative avenue for local authorities to raise revenue. In dealing with local authorities that it suspects of evading its controls, the Interior Ministry uses the sanction of delayed authorization. Delays can wreak havoc on the variety of financial and programmatic approvals that local officials require from the Interior Ministry. In an inflationary setting, a delayed authorization can be an expensive burden for the authority that receives it.

Local Authorities

In theory the financial policies of local authorities come from Israel's central government. Rates of local government taxes and service charges are either formally set or heavily influenced by government ministries. Local authorities also receive direct grants from national ministries. For 1981, these grants amounted to 59 percent of the local authorities' operating budgets. Eighty-five percent of their capital budgets in 1981 came as grants or loans from the central government.[18]

With all these signs of central domination, there is room for local maneuvering. Just as there are differences in budget status and style among the national ministries, so there are differences among the local authorities. Some opportunities come to local authorities because of the numerous links between them and national ministries. There is no single flow of revenue to local authorities via a national control point. Localities receive separate support from the Interior Ministry (a general grant); the Ministry of Education (for the support of schools plus youth and cultural programs); the Welfare Ministry (for local offices providing income support); the Ministry of Housing and Building (for local housing and public building projects); the Ministry of Transportation (for roads); and the Defense Ministry (for civil defense shelters). These ministries differ in the timing of their grants and the character of their supervision over local units. Local finance officers who are skillful in the management of cash find opportunities in these differences.

Personalities of mayors and senior staff of the municipalities, and their skills in exploiting opportunities are important in the Israeli budget process. The municipalities of Tel Aviv and Jerusalem provide remarkable examples. Tel Aviv is the Israeli city that most resembles an American metropolis. The central city with a population of 336,000 is surrounded by suburbs and satellites with some 1.4 million people. Tel Aviv is the commercial and cultural capital of the nation and serves numerous daily commuters who pay their local taxes elsewhere. The city's administration is the most sophisticated in the country and can bombard the capital with data that demonstrates the need for extraordinary aid. The city is also well aware of its demographic and economic importance and is not reluctant to flaunt national government regulations. Its budget strategy rests on its need to provide services to a large extraterritorial population, which will result in substantial indebtedness if the city is not awarded adequate aid.

Commercial banks recognize the city's importance, and are willing to extend credit on the assumption that the government must eventually come to the city's aid. As one Tel Aviv official explained the city's position, ''We offer Jerusalem the opportunity of aiding us before we cause a crisis of unpaid bills and unmet service needs, or after we cause that crisis.'' With Tel Aviv and the national government currently governed by similar party coalitions, the municipality's leaders also feel the advantage of political backing. However, Tel Aviv is not always successful in its relations with the central government. Under pressure from the government, for example, Tel Aviv cut more than one thousand workers in the 1980 to 1981 period.

The Jerusalem municipality benefits from its standing as the national capital and emotional center of Judaism. One item in the national budget awards Jerusalem an annual sum for being the capital. It is also policy for the separate ministries to favor Jerusalem in their projects. The government wants to make the city a model in transportation, hospital care, higher education, housing, and culture. The city is both a magnet for the tourist industry, and a site that is under international political scrutiny; the budget strategy of the municipality plays on these strengths. Its forte is the special status of Jerusalem, and the need for extraordinary government support. Its success is measured by its ability to avoid the substantial deficits that provide the leverage of Tel Aviv's budget strategy.

Israel's largest cities are not alone in playing budget games. In 1982 the categories of Arab towns, small towns, and development towns won special recognition in the national budget. They had convinced the Interior and Finance Ministries that their share of the municipalities' pie had eroded. Their argument gained strength by a series of municipal worker's strikes and public demonstrations. Small cities and development towns were excused from the Finance Ministry's mandate that all government budgets show a 5 percent cut in real terms from the previous budget. Arab towns won a budget increase of 10 percent in real terms.[19]

Stronger Management, Weaker Policy-Making

The Israeli budget remains a vital part of government machinery, despite an inflation rate that is among the world's highest. Part of the explanation lies in the character of Israeli inflation. Although the shekel's value changes daily, the currency has not collapsed. An extensive system of linkages to price increases, and continuous adjustments of the shekel's value in relation to foreign currency allow the budget process to continue as a tool of government. Critics question how long this can continue in the presence of a growing foreign debt. In the meantime, however, the budget has been strengthened in several ways as a tool of management. Via its accountant general's department, the Finance Ministry parcels out the resources to be allotted each spending unit for each of twelve monthly periods in the budget year. Along with the Interior Ministry and the Bank of Israel, the Finance Ministry has tightened the screws on local authorities. Now the Finance Ministry has stronger devices to control the number of local government personnel, and to keep local authorities from borrowing independently.

The most prominent strains in budgeting activities appear in policy planning. The Finance Ministry cannot decide once each year on the resources to be allocated to various purposes. Long-range or medium-range decision making is compromised by continuous adjustments. Not only are monthly allotments adjusted twelve times, but there are major budget exercises two or three times each year. On each of these occasions, pressures of the moment compete with goals established earlier. According to one participant, ''the pressing emergency overcomes the absolutely necessary.'' Program planning is described by participants as ''weakened'' or ''totally bankrupt.'' In such an atmosphere, technocrats express frustration. They are so harried by changing demands that they cannot concentrate on the careful analyses for which they are trained. What suffers, in particular, is the ability of the Finance Ministry to make the classic economic allocations between programs of competing value. Instead, the Ministry focuses on the simpler goal of using the budget process to restrain inflation.[20] There are lessons for bureaucratic politics in the Israeli budgeting situation. The Finance Ministry has sought to maintain or increase its control over spending units. It promoted some new linkages to the CPI and other automated decisions within the government sector (e.g., those applied to local authorities' taxes and service charges). Throughout the Begin era, the Finance Ministry resisted the application of "real cost" or "dollar-based" budgeting for government ministries. The finance minister preferred the more cumbersome system of midyear budget supplements and detailed allotment controls via the accountant general. Here the Finance Ministry could restrain and cut real growth in the spending of other ministries, outside the spotlight that would be applied to the single annual exercise of a real cost budget. Within the Finance Ministry, the standing of the accountant general increased along with the emphasis on "budgeting via the cash window." At the same time, the Budget Department, which prepared the original budget estimates, lost standing.

Budgeting remains political under high inflation. The behavior described here falls somewhere between that described for the United States with modest or low inflation,[21] and the frenzy of budgeting in poor countries.[22] Both the breadth of Israel's technocracy and the openness of its politics assure a budget process that is relatively sophisticated, even while it is harried by monetary values that change rapidly and bargains that must be restructured. Several of the tactics pursued by Israel's budget makers are similar to those observed by Wildavsky for the American cultural setting, with its more stable prices. At least some of the similarity is due to Aaron Wildavsky's impact on the education of public administrators since his classic study of budgeting appeared in 1964. Through his books, Wildavsky has taught budget-makers how to work and how to explain what they do. Perhaps a more basic reason for the similarity, however, is the generally competitive nature of government budgeting, and the commonalities that appear in participants' pursuit of advantages over their adversaries.

There are suggestions here for other countries. High inflation need not produce a collapse of the budget process if the most intense pressures associated with inflation (like eroded purchasing power and fear of collapse) are addressed by linkage mechanisms. In the public sector, the linkage of many items to price increase "automates" difficult decisions about taxes, service charges, interest, and spending. Without this simple solution for many pressing decisions, the mechanisms of financial control—including budgeting—might collapse from overload. Even with many such mechanisms in place, Israeli budget makers have had to adapt to changing circumstances. Basically, they have extended the system of decisions linked automatically to price increases, developed new flows of information, and tightened their controls over the managers of spending ministries.

Despite the budget adaptation of the Israeli Finance Ministry, disturbances associated with inflation remain. It is arguable as to whether the Ministry has tamed inflation; it clearly has not conquered it. Inflation remains at least a serious nuisance, and perhaps a major threat. The continuations of high inflation was one of the factors that contributed to the frustration and the resignation of Finance Minister Yoram Avidor. To his credit, however, the Israeli budget remained a viable tool of financial management throughout his administration.

CHAPTER 6

Governing the Holy City with a Private Budget

THE JERUSALEM FOUNDATION IS MAYOR TEDDY Kollek's device for coping with an official budget that is small and official procedures that are cumbersome. Jerusalem's special features, and the personal traits of Mayor and Foundation Chairman Kollek, go a long way in explaining the foundation's record of program accomplishments. At the same time, the foundation warrants general attention. Political scientists and economists elsewhere, as well as practicing politicians and administrators, have focused attention on the combined problems of resource shortages, and government bodies that commit themselves to more than they can deliver.[1] Among the remedies offered are nongovernmental providers of public services, and private philanthropy.[2] The Jerusalem Foundation is a successful example of a private body aiding government. It is also distinctive in its intimate relationship with the municipality, and illustrates some problems in the use of private resources by public officials. If other executives would seek to emulate Kollek, they had best consider the risks as well as the rewards.

THE JERUSALEM FOUNDATION: A DISTINCTIVE EXAMPLE OF AN ISRAELI PHENOMENON

While the positions of Teddy Kollek as head of both the Jerusalem Foundation and the municipality make this a special case, the Jerusalem Foundation also resembles many other bodies on the Israeli landscape. Universities, hospitals, museums, and countless other groups send their representatives abroad, or maintain offices overseas to solicit contributions. The Jewish Agency is the most conspicuous example in Israel of a body that depends financially on Jews in the Diaspora and reflects the influence of its biggest contributors and fund raisers in its policy-making organs.

The financial dependence on voluntary contributions from the Diaspora reflects both the tenuous financial position of modern Israel, and the long tradition of charity among Jews. For centuries before there was a state, Jews in the Diaspora sent money to Jewish institutions in Jerusalem and elsewhere in Israel.

It is difficult to remain for long in Jerusalem without coming to recognize the emblem that signifies contributions of the foundation. There have been over 600 Foundation-supported projects since 1966. The foundation is particularly committed to social and cultural programs, for both Arabs and Jews, and for poor neighborhoods. It has developed playgrounds and flower gardens in virtually every neighborhood. Theatres, tastefully designed, with active programs, offer subsidized productions for school children. Community centers have gymnasiums, sports fields, rooms for youth and adult education, dance, art workshops, and theatre. Parks, walkways, and amphitheatres appear at ancient landmarks, gracefully restored for modern purposes. Churches, mosques, and synagogues have been restored. A nineteenth century neighborhood has been developed into a work and housing site for visiting artists and intellectuals. There are subsidized workshops for young local artists, preschool centers and health clinics, traveling libraries, and attractive sculptures. In an Arab neighborhood, a health clinic, designed to suit both the architectural style and the service needs that prevail in that community, is currently nearing completion. The foundation supports archeological excavations and restorations. It has improved the infrastructure and services in the Old City by renovating buildings and streets, installing or repairing water, sewer, electric, and telephone lines, and providing cable television in order to eliminate unsightly antennas.

Foundation projects raise social and political issues in the delicate environment of Jerusalem. Religious, ethnic, and aesthetic sensitivities, with international reverberations, erupt over foundation proposals for certain building projects or the renovation of historical sites. Arab sensitivities about Jewish incursions appear even when foundation programs are directed at the physical or social problems of the Arab community. The sensitivities of religious Jews are at least as troublesome. Orthodox communities and their political parties have imposed stringent government control on prospective archaeological excavations, lest they disturb Jewish burial sites. Religious Jews have delayed or blocked foundation plans to construct sports and cultural facilities that are said to threaten the sensibilities or the Sabbath rest of religious neighborhoods.

The foundation's structure raises its own set of problems. Since 1966 Teddy Kollek has been mayor of the Jerusalem municipality and—in his private capacity—creator and chairman of the Jerusalem Foundation. With these dual roles, he has managed to override a governmental reform that the British accomplished some two hundred years ago. In a series of steps that included Edmund Burke's Civil Establishment Act of 1782, parliament separated the public resources of government from the private resources of the monarch, and asserted its own control over government.[3] In contemporary Jerusalem, Teddy Kollek can use the resources of his foundation to facilitate favorable decisions by municipal civil servants, the city council, and national government ministries. By earmarking foundation money for certain purposes, Kollek can persuade other officials to add government funds to those purposes. By directing the foundation to develop facilities in certain locales, Kollek can win the support of neighborhood residents and those members of the city council who represent them. In all of this, the publics of Jerusalem benefit from funds that originate outside of Israel, as private contributions. Often the procedures of the foundation are speedier than those of the municipality that operates with government money. To the extent that the foundation can avoid the procedures of government designed to keep public activities open to wide notice and participation, however, it also limits the accountability of public activity.

Organization and Finances

There are some fifty full-time employees at the foundation's headquarters in Jerusalem.[4] Elsewhere, affiliated foundations raise funds in the United States, the United Kingdom, Canada, and West Germany.

The formal structure of the Jerusalem Foundation resembles that of other nongovernmental, not-for-profit bodies. It meets the demands of reporting and auditing required by the laws of Israel and the countries of subsidiary foundations. In addition, the foundation and its subsidiaries have sought to assure the approval of its activities by the quality of public figures appointed to their councils.

The Jerusalem Foundation-Israel is headed by a council that is required to meet at least three times each year. Three to five members are chosen by the council for three-year terms to be the management committee. The chairman of the foundation is selected by the council for a five-year term, and also serves as chairman of the management committee. Formally, the management committee is the key decision-making body. It selects the manager of the foundation, the treasurer, and new members of the council, and defines the salaries, functions, and working conditions of foundation employees. In order to supervise the activities of the management committee, the council is required to select an accounts committee, not to include any member of the management committee; the accounts committee reviews annual reports of the foundation's chartered accountant.[5] The council's membership includes personalities from the highest levels of Israeli government, banking, and industry. Likewise, the councils of Jerusalem Foundations abroad include distinguished figures known for public service and philanthropy.

In practice, the moving forces of the foundation are its Chairman, Teddy Kollek, and its manager, Ruth Cheshin. Both have served in these positions since the foundation's inception in 1966. Both meet with donors, receive proposals from municipal agencies and other public bodies in Jerusalem, and oversee project planning and implementation.

Foundation officers define its status carefully with respect to the municipality. Laws and regulations of Israel, as well as those of donors' countries, prohibit or constrain formal links with the municipality. Israel's Interior Ministry (the supervisor of municipal government and finance) forbids private contributions to municipalities, per se. Tax authorities in the United States and Canada do not allow their residents to deduct from taxable income any donations to foreign governments, to programs that are mandated by foreign governments (like obligatory basic education), or to programs controlled by foreign governments. However, each of these authorities permits donations that enable the Jerusalem Foundation to support nonobligatory programs conducted in the framework of a municipal activity. Thus, the Foundation can subsidize theatre tickets that enable whole classrooms of primary school children to visit performances, insofar as this is not part of the curriculum required by the Ministry of Education.

The lines between permitted and prohibited activities are delicate. The foundation may support the construction of community centers (not required by government programs), but not the construction of primary schools. It may pay the costs of cultural programs suggested by personnel in the municipality—including programs that take place in school buildings—but not salaries of permanent municipal employees. Municipal officials have learned to formulate projects that fit within the foundation's constraints; they say that the foundation is likely to respond favorably if a proposal can be described as "new" or as a "supplement" to existing programs.

Officers of the foundation describe its financial worth as small in relation to other sources of public revenue; no simple standard exists by which this claim can be measured. However, the modesty seems exaggerated. For the 1966 to 1980 period, the foundation allocated $64 million. One standard for comparison is the municipal operating budget, which is itself made small by the substantial activities in Jerusalem financed directly by the Israeli central government. However, the operating budget reflects the public resources most readily controlled by the municipality. The foundation's annual outlays have been equal to some 16 percent of the municipal operating budget. This amount offers significant financial leverage to the mayor, without the more cumbersome procedures used for the allocation of government money.[6]

Mayor Teddy Kollek: King of Jerusalem?

The Jerusalem Foundation is an appendage of Teddy Kollek. He is a driving pragmatist, determined to get things done. When he speaks on the telephone, there may not be so much as a "shalom" (hello) before he barks questions or instructions. He is said to be on the streets by 6:00 A.M., checking on the city's gardeners and trash collectors. When he arrives at his office near the Jaffa Gate to the Old City, there may be visits or telephone calls with artists from abroad or national politicians. While waiting for an appointment, the author noted that Herman Wouk telephoned once and Shimon Peres twice. Kollek has governed Jerusalem for seventeen years, and is identified with the city in the media of both Israel and Western countries.

Kollek has a mixed reputation among those who work with him. He is quick with ideas and supports creative subordinates. He is a relentless if somewhat spasmodic pusher who can bulldoze an idea one day and forget it the next. Some subordinates think he is not a good implementer, claiming that he can be blind to the problems involved in putting his ideas into practice and reluctant to help when subordinates ask for support. One reported Kollek's desire to initiate cultural performances on Friday evening. The mayor proved unable or unwilling to deal with the opposition of orthodox religious communities concerned with preserving the Sabbath, and the project died.

Kollek is a master politician, as demonstrated by his long rule of a city beset with social tensions and political factions. He won yet another term in the municipal elections of 1983. He enjoys strong support from municipal administrators: "Is it good for Teddy?" is a prominent criteria among officials who consider projects that might be proposed to the foundation. If a project is good and is sponsored both by the Jerusalem Foundation and the municipality, it adds doubly to Kollek's stature and his ability to help administrators in return.

The Jerusalem Foundation is important to Kollek because it provides him with private resources—and thereby freedom—to operate in those aspects of local programming that he considers important. The mayor reports that he spends an hour or two every day on the business of the Jerusalem Foundation. He claims that he knows all the major donors, personally escorts them in Jerusalem, and visits them abroad. He conducts unveiling ceremonies for completed projects, where donors receive a gold medal set into a piece of the sandstone used for many of Jerusalem's buildings. His image of intimate involvement is useful to him and the foundation: his international reputation as the mayor of Jerusalem helps the foundation raise money; his local reputation as the chairman of the Jerusalem Foundation offers him leverage with municipal bureaucrats and council members who can advance his policies as mayor, and adds to his support among voters who benefit from foundation projects.

Virtually all sources had ready opinions about the eventual leadership transition, clearly a topic given much thought and discussion. There are competing prognoses. At the optimistic extreme is one scenario that is popular among employees of the foundation and municipal officials whose programs routinely receive its support. They see the foundation continuing as an independent entity, no matter who is mayor. The eternal attraction of Jerusalem will enable it to gather contributions, perhaps at amounts below those attracted by its star fundraiser-chairman-mayor. Its funds will enable the foundation to work with a mayor who does not have an intimate connection with it. Others describe an alternate scenario: the funds of the foundation will dry up once it loses Kollek as a prime attraction, and its capacity to implement programs will disappear once it loses the special leverage of the mayor's office with municipal planning and budget offices.

The Foundation Staff

The staff functions as an intermediary between donors and recipients. It maintains a file of prospective donors, including the kinds of projects they are apt to support. The foundation also hears continuously from municipal officials, personnel of other public bodies in Jerusalem, and private citizens with ideas they think merit support. Foundation personnel themselves formulate projects from general proposals they receive from prospective donors and recipients.

There are some fifty full-time employees of the foundation. Five work in public relations, concentrating on tours of Jerusalem for potential donors from abroad. Another five work with recipient agencies to plan cultural and social programs. Twelve persons comprise a technical staff, planning and implementing building projects. Staff architects design small projects, while outsiders, under contract, design larger projects. Four inspectors oversee projects in progress. Eight people work in the accounts department. Additional personnel fill posts of legal advisor, internal auditor, personnel manager, archivist, and general office workers.

The work of the staff varies with the issue at hand. Ideas may lie dormant for years until a suitable donor appears. If the foundation thinks that an idea is a sure winner, it may invest in site location, architectural sketches, and preliminary clearances from the municipality in order to speed up the process of finding a donor ready to make a commitment.

The staff produces an impressive array of publications to promote its past accomplishments and its offerings to potential donors. For large projects, there are glossy brochures with architectural sketches and descriptions of the proposed building or activity. Some projects are outlined in parts or stages, so that several donors can see their family name inscribed in Jerusalem. For projects that will take time between initial conception and the completion of various stages (and some have been in process for more than ten years), periodic newsletters describe accomplishments to date, and those in process.

Recipients of Foundation Support

Recipients play important roles in the work of the Jerusalem Foundation. Indeed, foundation officers assert that their own programming roles are minor. Most projects come initially as proposals from recipients and once a project is completed, the foundation leaves its management to them. For one of its projects (an academic research body named The Jerusalem Institute for Israel Studies), the foundation put the recipients in contact with their own overseas donor, who now provides continuing independent support.

The typical recipient of foundation funds is a government body or private organization staffed by professionals in cultural programming or social services. At times, however, citizen clients approach the foundation. Such was the case when a group of parents requested a playground especially designed for their handicapped children. The foundation organized contacts with municipal departments who would provide programming; sought out an appropriate site; initiated clearance procedures with city planning agencies; arranged for architectural sketches and estimates; and then approached donors.

The Municipality

Officers of the Jerusalem municipality have a say in many of the foundation's projects. Projects that entail land acquisition and/or construction must obtain approvals from planning and engineering units. In cases of grants to municipal departments, such as education, or youth, culture, and sport, program officers in those departments help define the character of foundation projects. Whenever a project entails a financial commitment by the municipality for infrastructure, or supplemental programming, the municipal budget department enters the picture.

There are three competing views about the quality of the municipal reviews given to foundation projects. First there is Teddy Kollek's simple assertion: projects that require municipal approval must pass through the formal procedures; discussion closed! Second, and at another extreme, is a response from foundation antagonists. They assert that the mayor railroads approval for foundation projects through municipal procedures; that he overcomes opposition with the leverage of foundation resources; and that much of the foundation's activities are hidden from the scrutiny of the public or political scientists. When asked for specifics, such antagonists retreat to the protection of their own argument: the true facts remain hidden in the closed circle where the mayor is also chairman of the foundation. A third view tends to be expressed by municipal officials who must review foundation proposals. They admit that foundation projects receive special treatment. At the same time they assert that such projects are subject to significant municipal control. They point to projects that are turned down or altered because of opposition from budget, planning, or engineering departments. The engineering department has issued formal stop-work orders on foundation construction projects.[7]

How do we explain the claim of municipal controls over foundation projects on the one hand and the admission of special treatment on the other? The character of the mayor's power is important, as is the character of the mayor himself. He is the central figure in the municipality. When he is further bolstered by access to significant independent funding, he can exert leverage on officials who might object to his projects. Further, he can be outspoken and harsh. Subordinates perceive that he does not like opposition to the details of foundation projects; some fear his explosive outbursts. At the same time, the municipal bureaucracy has an important layer of professional budgeters, planners, and engineers. Along with a certain amount of job protection, these people know how to activate interested members of the city council or the media. The mayor cannot lightly dismiss their objections to foundation projects. Furthermore, he recognizes and respects the limits of his personal freedom. He has worked to maintain an untainted image for himself and his foundation. This means that he rejects certain donors and certain projects as being outside the realm of good taste and backs off from projects that generate intense objections.

Municipal officials have a substantial reservoir of respect and even admiration for the foundation. They recognize it as an important supplement to government funds, and they do what they can to facilitate its proposals. Pragmatists in the city budget department allow program departments to shift municipal funds from one category to another, in order to mesh them with the funds that the foundation is able to provide. Generally, the budget department satisfies itself with the bottom line of annual expenditures. As long as a program unit does not exceed its total allocation, it need not follow the letter of initial projections as to how much it will spend for which programs. Professionals in the city engineering unit also look with favor on foundation proposals. Informally, they put them in a category with projects of other public bodies, without the close attention to the formal procedures that are imposed on profit-oriented private contractors. There is, in other words, respect for the foundation and a presumed acceptance of its proposals. At one time the Engineering Department was even more tolerant; it allowed the foundation to proceed with extensive excavation and buildings, prior to formal clearance of its plan. Now procedures are more strictly enforced, but the foundation is still given more leeway in getting projects underway than is permitted to private construction.

The fate of one former city manager suggests the outer limits of overt opposition to foundation projects that may come from the city bureaucracy. In Teddy Kollek's Jerusalem, the post of city manager is subordinate to that of mayor. The manager typically handles the administration of city affairs, while the mayor engages in policy-making and dabbles in administration when he feels it appropriate. Roni Feinstein came to the post of manager after a career as a military officer. He played a role in policy determination, and was called "Teddy's golden boy" and "likely successor." With the Jerusalem Foundation, however, he overstepped his bounds and met his match. For awhile it was Feinstein against Ruth Cheshin, manager of the foundation. Feinstein sought to assert the full extent of municipal review procedures over foundation projects, and a more complete disclosure of foundation affairs; Cheshin sought autonomy for the foundation, and a speedy implementation of its projects. Both appealed to the mayor for support, and Cheshin won. Later, Feinstein left the municipality to practice law.

One issue in relations between the municipality and the foundation is maintenance costs. This is a perennial problem of bodies financed partly by donations. While contributors are proud to construct something that will carry their name, they are less than eager to pay for its upkeep.

The explicit policy of the Jerusalem Foundation is that the municipality or other recipients of its funds must commit themselves to maintain the facility. From the municipality's perspective, officials admit to concern about the issue. The growing number of parks and buildings that carry the foundation imprimatur must be cleaned, kept in repair, and serviced with staff and utilities. Opponents of the foundation are even more explicit: they charge that the need to supplement foundation contributions with maintenance costs significantly distorts the priorities that would be defined by a completely independent municipality. In fact, the foundation is not oblivious to the issue of maintenance. It wants to keep alive the facilities it has built; many of its grants support programming in community centers, theatres, and outdoor exhibition sites. When viewed in general terms, the foundation does contribute significantly to the ongoing maintenance of Jerusalem's facilities.

Donors

The Jerusalem Foundation would be nothing without its donors. Not only do they provide its resources, they also shape its programs. Most donors want to know what they are supporting. They also want the residents of Jerusalem—and other friends back home—to know who supported a given program. There is little by way of unspecified or anonymous contributions. People who want to aid Israel without everlasting credit can do so through the United Jewish Appeal in the United States or the United Israel Appeal in other countries.

Some donors are well-versed in the programs they support. They show an interest in program planning, follow the progress of their project, and may help with additional contributions for later stages. Other donors have at least a general idea of what they will support and rely on the foundation to suggest something specific. Still others are interested primarily in putting their name on a piece of Jerusalem. As one foundation employee said, "Some donors can talk intelligently for hours about the details of programming. Others can talk for hours only about the size of letters that will indicate their support, and which family members should be listed on the dedication."

Jerusalem and Teddy Kollek are central to the foundation's fund-raising strategy. Most pledges are finalized in a tour of the city. For some prospective donors, Teddy Kollek is the tour guide. For many more, he is one of the sights included in the tour. Lower ranking staff members, and per-

sonnel in branch foundations overseas help to prepare donors and see to the actual transfer of funds.

The typical donor is a Jew whose resources come from
a family-owned business. However, there are significant
donations from non-Jews who are attracted by the magic of
Jerusalem, its significance in international affairs, the projects of the foundation, or the charm of Teddy Kollek. Not
all offerings are accepted by the foundation. Some are rejected on grounds of bad taste and some in order to preserve the reputation of the organization for honest dealing.
The foundation has rejected proposals to help prospective
donors with tax problems in a foreign country by exaggerat-
ing reports of donations, in exchange for part of the profits.
It seeks to protect itself from the image of selling the favors
of the municipality by not making a practice of soliciting
contributions from Israelis. And the foundation is especially wary of donors who might expect licenses or contracts from the municipality. For this reason, it claims to
refuse donations offered by building contractors.

Almost all foundation publications appear exclusively
in English. According to foundation officers, this indicates
the focus of foundation efforts on North America and the
United Kingdom and its policy to discourage donations
from Israelis.

How It All Comes Together—Or Doesn't

Issues involved in major building projects illustrate the
physical and political problems of Jerusalem, and the inter-
actions of the mayor, the foundation's staff, municipal departments, and donors. Site locations can offer major challenges. The staff must find physically available land, in a
suitable location, whose ownership is clear, and whose intended use is not likely to arouse intractable opposition.
The staff also must obtain permits from municipal planning

and engineering authorities. Other commitments must come from programming departments to make use of the facility as intended by the donor or from the municipal budget unit to contribute to the costs of construction or operation. It is at these stages that the mayor's help can be indispensable.

Occasionally, even the mayor is not sufficient. In one instance, the foundation was a party, with several other groups, to the construction of a new sports stadium that encountered the unbending opposition of the city's orthodox Jewish communities. This issue was settled against the project at the highest levels of national politics, by the prime minister and the minister of the interior. Yet another project, planned for the Jewish Quarter of the Old City, has dragged on for twelve years with a series of delays. First there was a need to proceed slowly and in collaboration with archaeologists of the Israeli Antiquities Department, which is concerned that no relics be destroyed or permanently hidden from exploration. Next came protests from the religious community that the proposed amphitheatre would disturb nearby religious institutions. As part of the protests, a religious party withdrew from the mayor's coalition in the city council. The project is now defined as a garden rather than an amphitheatre. It is still not completed, and the original donors have abandoned it in frustration.

SIGNIFICANCE

The Jerusalem Foundation is an important actor in local government. It contributes prominently to the physical development of Jerusalem, to its extensive cultural programs, and to its social services. It receives special treatment from municipal departments dealing with physical planning, engineering, and budgeting.

The foundation reflects the special character of Jerusalem. There may be no other city that so stimulates the emotions and pocketbooks of foreigners who are under no obligation to help local authorities with their financial problems. Yet, Jerusalem did not create the foundation. Teddy Kollek recognized the potential of his city to attract contributors and built the foundation into an organization that allows him to operate significantly beyond the capacity of his government budget. The option is open to others who govern places that might attract private support.

The Jerusalem Foundation also reflects conditions that prevail generally in Israel. There are important roles for organizations whose financial bases are nongovernmental or foreign. The Histadrut provides important social services; its General Sick Fund's comprehensive health service enrolls 80 percent of the population. The Jewish Agency receives donations from abroad and administers a number of social programs. Hospitals, universities, schools, and religious and cultural institutions solicit from their own donors, as well as from the Histadrut, the Jewish Agency, and government ministries. Yet no other body quite resembles the Jerusalem Foundation. The thorough mixture of public and private roles, as played by Teddy Kollek, is unique on the contemporary Israeli stage.[8]

There is ample evidence from Western democracies that private and public bodies may coexist with mutual advantages. Programs supported by the Jerusalem Foundation are widely used and admired. However, Teddy Kollek's mixing of private and public roles makes it impossible to establish the accountability of the Foundation's role in municipal affairs. Its projects are not subject to standard procedures of review because the officials charged with review have to deal with its chairman in his other role as mayor.

There is no evidence of what an American muckraker would call "dishonest graft"[9] surrounding Teddy Kollek or the Jerusalem Foundation. Interviews with a range of participants, observers, and antagonists turn up nothing more than clouded allegations of selling favors or influencing municipal priorities. Articles about the foundation in the Israeli press, including a local newspaper with an inclination to exposé, rely more on hints than substance.[10] From the look of things, it is not possible to accuse Teddy Kollek of anything more tangible than a driving pragmatism that is not sufficiently attuned to the implications of his peculiar role as foundation chairman and city mayor.

Occasionally, one hears Kollek labeled the "king of Jerusalem." In the contentious politics of Jerusalem and Israel, there is little danger than his kingly stature will have any importance beyond the metaphor. As in real monarchies, the real test will come with his passing. No monarchical succession appears on the horizon, even though Kollek is well into his seventies. Foundation personnel worry about the succession. There is some question as to whether the organization can survive at all without Kollek, beyond the exhaustion of its capital reserves and outstanding pledges. At the least, the senior staff will have to scramble in order to retain their income from donors and their clout in the city administration. One wonders if the foundation can maintain its present influence without a mayor-chairman identified both with the city and the foundation.

Entrepreneurial officeholders may find several implications in this discussion of the Jerusalem Foundation. First, a place or program may require a certain magic to attract significant voluntary donations. Not many places may stir the emotions of potential donors like Jerusalem. However, donations do come elsewhere in response to attractive presentations of publicly managed social or cultural activities. Second, even modest private funds may expand their weight via the leverage they offer. An executive with access to donations may extract additional funds from the jurisidiction's legislature and from other jurisdictions above his on the national hierarchy. Third, there are tricky issues where private donations enter the public sector. The foundation abides by the requirements imposed on private

fund-raising bodies. These procedures do not open foundation activities to public scrutiny and participation to the same extent as requirements imposed on the municipality and other public bodies.

Kollek's personalization of the linkage between the Jerusalem Foundation and the municipality has exposed him to charges of operating outside the realm of political accountability and may endanger the foundation's capacity to survive a transition in the mayor's office. On the other hand, the intimate linkage between a hard-driving foundation chairman/municipal chief executive helps in using private resources as leverage with officials who control public resources, and appealing to donors as a foundation that can get things done. This case from Jerusalem suggests a trade-off of accountability versus dispatch in the institutionalization versus personalization of a private-public linkage. Where the emphasis is placed on personalization, the key person must be sensitive to those who would exploit the linkage in order to buy favors from public officeholders. The political setting of Jerusalem features free competition, active media, and a well-developed sense of political morality. Should there develop a substantial hint of influence-peddling, it could foul the magic that is necessary for private donations to a public body.

CHAPTER 7

Problems of Program Implementation

PEOPLE HAVE COMPLAINED ABOUT THEIR GOV-
ernments for centuries. They have found their kings and
ministers corrupt or incompetent. Taxes have been intoler-
able. Government permission to engage in certain activities
has been granted at the cost of great delay, arbitrary controls, or overt favoritism. Social services such as education,
medical care, housing, and income security have developed only recently in the history of governments and have
given rise to complaints about unfair distributions to various regions and population groups and staff personnel
who lack adequate training or motivation for their work.

GOVERNMENT PROGRAMS IN MODERN TIMES

The spread of democracy and the elevation of living standards in the nineteenth and twentieth centuries improved

the quality of government services and, at the same time, complaints directed at government became increasingly sophisticated. The mass media now add their own skills of analysis to these complaints. Governments themselves have joined the complainers, perhaps to avoid the charge that they are uncaring in the presence of an active electorate. The supreme audit units of several countries have gone beyond their traditional concern for financial accounting, and have probed the performance of programs for effectiveness, efficiency, and the overall wisdom of their conception. Added to this, the proliferation of ombudsmen provides the common citizen with a governmental organ for protection against the improper imposition of burdens, or improper exclusion from governmental benefits.

The academic discipline of political science has long been in the forefront of those concerned with the functions of government. It has described and analyzed the activities of elected officials and administrative bodies. Along with other contributions, academics have exposed corrupt leaders and ill-conceived programs, and have sought to improve election mechanisms, civil service selection and training, policy-making, and program implementation.

In recent years academics have focused attention on the failure of programs to be implemented in the ways conceived by program advocates. The literature on *implementation* actually focuses on the *failures* of implementation.[1] If there is a prevalent fault in the writing on program implementation, it lies in the implications that programs tend not to work in a desirable fashion. As a corrective, it is appropriate to assert that most programs do work more or less as intended, most of the time. By all appearances, for example, programs of traffic control in Israel and elsewhere succeed in leading most cars to drive on the proper side of the road at or below the legal speed limit. Most citizens entitled to old-age insurance receive their payments on time and for the proper amounts. Programs of national financial aid to schools and universities distribute most of their budget allocations according to the procedures written in laws or regulations. A more complicated issue is whether such financial aids succeeds in meeting the goals for quality education that appear in the aspirations of policy-makers and citizens.

Certain kinds of programs seem least vulnerable to problems of implementation: programs that are old and well established, that are simple for administrators and clients to comprehend, and that do not provoke sharp political controversies. In contrast are the programs that seem *most vulnerable* to problems of implementation. These are programs that are new, that demand administrators and/or clients to depart from customary patterns of behavior, that are complex and difficult for both administrators and clients, and/or that provoke continuing disputes among politicians and interest groups.

Defining the Problems of Implementation

The lapses in program implementation that occur in Israel reflect the special traits of its society and government, as well as general problems that occur in many societies. Israeli wits say that Jews are just like any other people, only more so. The state they have created reflects the history of a people who had no governmental experience for nearly two thousand years. It may be the burden of Zionism that Jews should be governed only by other Jews or that only Jews should face the task of governing Jews. Perhaps every country is unique. However, Israel may be more unique than most other countries. There is much in the small state of four million people to tax the ingenuity of all who would comprehend or cope with its program implementation problems. The general problems of Israeli administration result from the ethnic and religious complexities of Jewish cultures, convoluted governmental structure, and a lack of fit between resources that are severely limited and demands for programs that are enlarged by the appetites of Israelis and the determination of their enemies.

Israel's problems of program implementation fall into three classifications. First is a group that reflects the underlying tensions of Israeli society and government. These are the problems that derive most clearly from the special traits of Israel. Second are problems that appear in governments throughout the world. They may be exaggerated somewhat in Israel. However, observers in other countries may also feel they are worse there. In bureaucracy as in private life, the grass tends to look greener elsewhere. Third are problems that reflect a customary lack of awareness about program implementation as a general problem of policymaking.

GROUP I: PROBLEMS REFLECTING THE DISTINCTIVE TRAITS OF ISRAEL

Lack of Coordination

Many governments encounter problems of coordination. Ministries and departments are established at one point in time, often along lines of demarcation developed elsewhere and considered conventional. Education, defense, transportation, health, justice, interior, welfare, and communications are the most common. As programs develop, it becomes evident that they cross the boundaries of two or more units; this often causes problems. Questions arise about the division of responsibility and resources. Bureaucratic units develop perspectives of their own, and their members seek to expand their powers or resources. *Bureaucratic imperialism*[2] leads to battles with paper, meetings, and telephone calls as one unit's struggle for aggrandizement threatens another's terrain. Even in the absence of open warfare, it is necessary to arrange communication across administrative boundaries with care and delicacy. With the best of motives, differences in perspectives may obscure the meaning of program guidelines, and units may embark in contrary directions.

The Israeli setting magnifies each of these problems. In addition to the conventional problem of coordination across ministries, major programs require the coordination of government bodies with the Histadrut, the Jewish Agency, or organizations of Jewish communities abroad. Government-Histadrut frictions have been especially tense since 1977, while Likud has controlled the government and Labour has controlled the Histadrut. Relations between a government unit and a community in the Diaspora can also be delicate. While an Israeli unit might have its own plans, a proud donor or fund raiser abroad may have a strong and different sense of what to do with the money gathered.

The first years of Project Renewal illustrate the problems of faulty coordination that seem endemic to Israel. Project Renewal is a program to improve buildings and social services in selected neighborhoods. It was conceived to deal with a problem that has deep roots in Israel's short history. Part of the problem comes from the social disadvantages of families that immigrated in the late 1940s and 1950s; poverty, inadequate education, and large numbers were combined with the physical problems of finding or creating housing. At various times the newcomers were crowded into tents or other temporary dwellings and, ultimately, to the urban neighborhoods deserted by Arabs who fled from the war of independence or into neighborhoods built as quickly and as cheaply as possible by the new state. The problems of this population appeared on the government agenda continuously beginning in the late 1940s.

Project Renewal built upon the base of existing housing and social programs for distressed neighborhoods. However, several new twists distinguished it from its predecessors and destined it for problems of implementation. It was identified by the prime minister as a keystone of his government's social programs and as a key feature of Israel's relations with Jewish communities in the Diaspora. He and other senior ministers made it the focus of fund-raising missions abroad. To heighten its appeal, the prime minister targeted individual neighborhoods as the direct responsibility of communities abroad. The Jews of Chicago, Montreal, Los Angeles, and elsewhere ''adopted'' Israeli neighborhoods. Deputy Prime Minister Yigal Yadin accepted responsibility for Project Renewal as the key program in his portfolio for social policy.

It is worth noting that the deputy prime minister had an extensive base of personal political support after the election of 1977. However, the locus of his personal strength lay in middle- and upper-income neighborhoods with higher than average levels of education. These were not the communities to be served by Project Renewal. The program itself was loaded down with several goals, both procedural and substantive: to involve the residents of the poor neighborhoods, as well as Diaspora donors and Israeli government officials in program planning and execution; to deal with the physical problems of crowding, inadequate housing, and other community facilities; to improve the social condition of neighborhood residents with programs of counseling plus educational and cultural enrichment. The organizations with a role in the program included the Jewish Agency; the Israeli ministries of the prime minister, finance, housing and construction, welfare and labor, education and culture, plus the Israel Lands Authority, municipalities, and various housing companies owned by the Israeli government, the municipalities, and the Jewish Agency.

All told, Project Renewal was destined to be a rich stew of organizational and personal motives. From the Diaspora were donors who simply wanted to contribute to the improvement of Israel's social conditions and to rely on others to define programs that would lead to improvement. Other donors relied on Israeli organizations to define policy, but did not trust them to act with dispatch. They wanted to sit with policy-makers, administrators, and neighborhood residents and to nudge them along. Yet other donors wanted to define the policies for their adopted neighborhoods and perhaps to battle with Israeli organizations or neighborhood residents in order to see their goals accomplished.

Each Israeli organization has its own concerns. For them, Project Renewal has come on the scene after many years of experience and perspectives. Depending on the principal tasks of an organization, Project Renewal represents opportunities to deal more effectively with urban land use, the construction of housing and other physical facilities, or improved social programming in the fields of education, family counseling, youth groups, or community centers. Along with all of these goals, there are considerable stakes for individual prestige. Leaders of Diaspora communities, Israeli mayors, ministers, and vocal community residents all want to make a distinctive imprint on a project to be sure that their constituencies see that they are playing a major role. There is ample opportunity for the theatrics of grand proposals, empassioned speeches, and dogged obstructionsism.

Israel's state comptroller has reviewed Project Renewal several times.[3] Among his early findings were a number of observations that reflected the absence of designated participants from decision making, or a lack of coordination among the participants:

- failure by units appointed to coordinate projects to meet or to carry out their designated tasks;
- failure of designated mechanisms to transfer funds in a timely fashion from the Jewish Agency—which re-

ceived them from Diaspora communities—to the Israeli Treasury for disbursement to program administrators;

- failure to include local government authorities on the
teams appointed to designate particular neighborhoods for inclusion in the program;
- failure to meet the announced goals of including
neighborhood residents in program planning and execution; and
- lack of progress by social rehabilitation programs that
were to accompany programs of physical rehabilitation.

Reading between some lines of the state comptroller's
reports, we can find a dilemma. The state comptroller faults
program administrators for failure to meet the goals of improving the representativeness of decision making, especially with respect to increasing the voice of municipal authorities and neighborhood residents, and for insufficient
central record keeping, program monitoring, and program
implementation. On the surface, the goals of greater representativeness on the one hand and greater dispatch plus
more effective central controls on the other hand appear
contradictory. If the representatives of various participants
are more active, they will likely produce more problems of
coordination for central authorities and greater problems of
planning and completing projects in a speedy fashion.

The state comptroller's report on Magen David Adom
(the equivalent of the Red Cross) published in 1979
presents another variety of a coordination problem.[4] Magen David Adom is the provider of first aid in Israel. It is
prone to uneven waves of international support. During
and immediately after wartime, the organization receives
more contributions from abroad than it can absorb effi-
ciently. There is also a tendency toward independence
among the local branches of Magen David Adom. Local
units establish separate links with groups of overseas do-

nors, and acquire facilities and equipment out of step with the national planning of Magen David Adom's central office. At times the national organization finds itself saddled with demands to support a facility begun by a local chapter with the help of overseas donors, where the local chapter lacks an adequate assessment of the need for the facility or sufficient Israeli funds to make its required contribution.

Administrative Overload

It is tempting for governments to stretch their resources. Often they try to do several things at the same time. A ministry may add longstanding plans to a new program that enjoys political favor. In other words, it seeks to climb onto a new horse with some old programs. The problem comes when too many units seek to attach themselves to an attractive program. The load of all their extra requests may doom the entire program to failure, including both its major goals and all the surplus that has been added.[5]

Israel may be more prone than other countries to the problem of administrative overload. The lack of symmetry between extensive aspirations and limited resources presents numerous situations in which officials are tempted to stretch resources by adding their own goals to the programs of other ministries. Also, a cultural instinct to improvise finds a hospitable setting in civilian as well as military agencies. To make do with limited resources is a prized national tradition. It threatens program goals, however, when it is pushed too far by officials who are oblivious to the borders beyond which a program's security will be jeopardized.

A classic case of administrative overload came on the heels of the Camp David peace treaty with Egypt. In order to accommodate the treaty's provisions of Israeli withdrawal from the Sinai, the military planned to relocate major installations to the Negev. This commanded first place on the nation's agenda. The peace treaty was a break-through in Israel's relations with its Arab neighbors. Israel could not delay the scheduled withdrawal of military forces from the Sinai. Neither could the government delay repositioning its crucial bases. The Israeli military, and not the peace treaty, would continue as the ultimate guarantee of the nation's safety.

With a program of such unchallenged importance, it is not surprising that others found a way to climb on the bandwagon. Civilian ministries saw the opportunity to further long-standing goals of increasing the population of the Negev. Development towns in the region saw the opportunity to improve their housing and road connections. There was planning to develop industry and tourism. Against all this activity, groups and agencies concerned with the natural environment sought to protect the scenery and ecology of the Negev. If all such goals were not contradictions in pure logic, they became contradictory due to the pressure of limited time and funds. The state comptroller examined the program, and found several problems. Behind the items on the following list, we can see a program that suffered from too many aspirations for the resources—including time—made available, and was compelled to sacrifice certain goals as policy-makers and administrators faced reality:[6]

- lack of planning and implementation of several goals not directly connected with the transfer of the military installations, such as road improvements, development of services in towns, establishment of projects for industry, agriculture, and tourism, and creation of nature reserves.
- shortage in the completion of projected needs for housing, estimated at 42 percent of units needed by the end of 1982.
- few efforts to include representatives of the region's local authorities in program planning or execution.

Violation of Orderly Structures and Procedures

It is tempting for governments, like individuals, to take shortcuts. If an opportunity presents itself, there are pressures to exploit it, quickly; delay may see the opportunity disappear. To consult with all the parties having a legitimate concern in an activity will take time, and may allow one of the parties to detour or veto the project that is envisioned. The pressure to take a shortcut may be especially acute in Israel, with its shortage of resources, its surplus of aspirations, and its governmental structures that are all too complex.

While the appeal of a shortcut may be a quick fix to a difficult problem, the effort may go awry. The hiker who attempts a shortcut may lose his way, and spend great time and energy finding the correct path. There may be tragedies, as when a shortcut leads to an abyss. Likewise in government. The pursuit of an attractive opportunity by means of improper structures and procedures can create administrative monsters that are more foreboding than what might have resulted from the use of cumbersome, but legitimate procedures in the first instance. One such example appears in the story of the Tel Aviv bus station.

The original problem of the Tel Aviv municipality was one that troubles officials the world over: how to develop a major public facility, conveniently located in the heart of a large and congested metropolitan area, that will demand extensive changes in land use. Not only is there the issue of huge financial cost for land-taking, clearing, and construction, but there are additional problems of dislocating existing residential and business occupants and dealing with the individual and community protests that are bound to erupt. [7]

The Tel Aviv municipality sought to shortcut the problems by availing itself of a deal with a private investor, who offered a sizable plot of land in an area that seemed suitable to the venture. A company was created by the private investor, who assumed 50 percent of the shares, a construction company of the Histadrut, with 15 percent of the shares, and the transportation cooperative Egged, with 35 percent of the shares. The plans included not only the structures integral to intercity and intracity bus transportation and conveniences for travelers, but also a commercial complex of shops, restaurants, banks, and other facilities that would draw customers from the huge daily flow of people through the bus station. The rent from these facilities promised sizable profits to the investors. For its part, the municipality agreed to provide road connections for the bus station. The basic construction of the bus station occurred during the years 1968 to 1975, but the facility is not yet connected to the road system. A huge edifice stands useless and crumbling in the heart of Israel's major city, a landmark to planning gone awry.

The story of the failure is long and complex. Among its central features, however, was the failure of the municipality to take proper account of the costs involved in clearing the area needed for access roads—an area several times the size of the bus station itself—including compensations to be paid to the many owners and occupants of existing structures. There remain charges that the basic planning was faulty; that without the prospect of land already assembled (for the building itself), no decision would have been taken to locate such a land-hungry structure in such a crowded neighborhood.

There have been several proposals for dealing with the project. Meanwhile, residents of the neighborhood continue to suffer from the uncertainty of not knowing when they will have to vacate and under what conditions of compensation. Private investors in the bus station, plus the Histadrut construction firm of Solel Boneh and the Egged bus cooperative, have lost considerable sums, as have the many firms and individuals that acquired commercial space in the as yet unused building. Moreover, travelers remain with an eyesore in place of the efficient central bus station they were promised years ago. The Israeli public may be the greatest loser, having to pay the bill to set right what was done wrong.

The Tel Aviv bus station illustrates the variety of public organizations that are supervised loosely, if at all, and suggests the merits of tightening supervision by the central government. At the other extreme, a government company to search for petroleum encountered procedures of supervision that were unduly strict. Professionals and technicians in the company could not use their skills freely in the pursuit of company goals. The government itself set policy, with little freedom allowed even for the directors appointed by the government to oversee the company.[8] Apparently, the economic and political importance of petroleum heightened the government's involvement in the details of this company's operations. The golden mean of proper autonomy can be distorted by too little as well as too much administrative freedom.

GROUP II: PROBLEMS SHARED BY ISRAEL AND OTHER COUNTRIES

Israel is a country with many distinctive and fascinating traits that contribute to its difficulties in program implementation. At the same time, Israel is a country like many others in the world; it suffers from problems of administration that are prosaic and universal. However, the universal character of these problems should not blind critics to their importance. While some aspect of them may always appear in a review of government activities, they can be lessened in frequency or in their negative impact on the quality of gov-

ernment activities. To describe their existence is to take a
first step toward protecting programs from their influence.

Inadequate Resources of Money and/or Personnel

A common explanation for the failure of government programs to meet their targets is inadequate resources. The
lack of sufficient resources may reflect a sheer insufficiency
of resources to meet public demands for services or the in-
ability of planners to predict the costs of a program or its
personnel needs. For new programs, the finding of insufficient resources may reflect pressures against coming in
with figures that are too high at early stages of program
planning. Administrators who fear killing a program by es-
timating its true costs, however, may doom it to frustration
by offering a budget that is politically acceptable but too low
for adequate program development.

The telecommunications service in Israel is chronically
behind in its efforts to meet public demand. Delays of five
years and more between customer requests and telephone
service are not unusual. An obvious explanation is insufficient resources. There is the classic quandry of allocation:
how much of the public's resources should policy-makers
allocate to the immediate satisfaction of service demands in
any one field? However, the citation of limited resources
may be too easy an explanation for some problems in the
telephone service. The state comptroller's annual report for
1979 cites the ministry of communications for failing to
keep up with schedules commensurate with the levels of
funding and personnel actually provided.[9]

Investigations into court proceedings and the police
have also raised resource questions. One report indicated
that court activities suffered considerable delay because the
routing procedures were overloaded and clogged. There
were insufficient court personnel to handle the cases. An-

other report indicated that the police could not handle the increasing number of criminal investigations due to too few police personnel and vehicles and too little training of investigators.[10]

The state comptroller's inquiry into the police department's lack of success in dealing with sophisticated and organized crime suggests that the simple assertion of insufficient resources might hide more than it reveals. Money by itself does not solve social problems. Rather, the wise allocation of available funds and attention to staff selection and training may make up for some deficiencies in resources. Also, the lack of wise budget allocations or of attention to recruitment and training may doom a well-budgeted program to failure. One of the police problems cited by the state comptroller was a lack of adequate training for its personnel. Another was a considerable gap in the percentage of budgeted positions actually filled.[11]

Conflicts Between Program Goals

The problem of contradictory goals results from policy-makers who want to have their cake and to eat it too. Sometimes planners elevate contradictory platitudes to the level of policy objectives. This was the case in a document circulated to ministries by the Civil Service Commission in July 1980. The document's most prominent message was its call to improve the quality of public service. At the same time, however, the Civil Service Commission indicated that there was to be no increase in budget or other resources. In fact, there is much experience to suggest that the serious pursuit of program goals requires money and other resources in redundant amounts.[12] Saving money is a virtue only if pursued in proper proportion and context. No one should tolerate the profligate waste of resources that do not produce results commensurate with their value. Yet tight-fisted policy-makers or administrators are also wasteful. If the resources spent are not sufficient to attain their objectives, they are as profligate as those who spend at excess, with no concern for the products obtained. The Civil Service Commission's own circular suggested the limits of its utility. Many of its examples of service improvements were described in very general terms, suggesting that the policies were not being taken seriously by those who authored them.

Excessive Reliance on Reorganization

There are many formulas in the literature of public administration that allege advantages from such organizational structures as government companies, independent authorities, or other units separate from the conventional ministries. Still other formulas tout the benefits of central control, with close supervision of service providers by key administrators. In truth, however, the formal structure of an organization is only one among many of the factors that influence the performance of its workers. Often organizational structure is weak in the face of other influences, such as the level of financing, the numbers and quality of staff, the character of clients (clients with moderate problems are easier to serve than those with complex and severe problems), or the morale of the staff. To initiate a change in one factor that may affect services (i.e., organizational structure) without ensuring the improvement of all the other factors may invite frustration. Moreover, the price of frustration is likely to be high. Organizational change in itself is costly in terms of time; it involves the preparation of management, employees, and clients; the suspicions generated at all levels by such change; and the compensations demanded by employees in exchange for dislocated schedules, careers, or work places.

Through organizational change, Israel perenially attacks the issue of emigration. One report of the state comptroller found that a new unit of the ministry of immigration and absorption had failed to deal adequately with its tasks in its first year of operation.[13] Perhaps there was not sufficient time for the organization to get its programs underway. It is more likely, however, that the underlying economic and social causes of emigration in individual cases are too deeply rooted for facile treatment by changing the structures of government units.

Insufficient Authority

It is a platitude of "good management" that responsibility must be coupled with authority. The administrator must have the wherewithall to accomplish what is expected. Often, however, officials do not have sufficient power to carry out their assigned tasks. This problem is closely related to that of insufficient resources, as when officials have insufficient authority to spend money or hire personnel up to the demands of their program responsibilities.

As a distinct problem, however, "insufficient authority" refers to a program officer who lacks the power to compel others—subordinates, other agencies, citizens, business firms—to act in accord with program requirements. The problem may result from policy-makers who like the sound of a program but do not like it so much that they grant it sufficient independence, sufficient resources, or sufficient legal authority to compel citizens or business firms to accept its regulations. The result is a program that is symbolic only, without the muscle to accomplish its goals. Israeli environmental protection programs, like those of other countries, have yet to receive sufficient authority to carry out their assigned tasks. The natural environment is sufficiently attractive, apparently, to gain symbolic recognition from policy-makers, but not sufficiently important for its agencies to receive enough power to deal effectively with the competing demands of economic development, employment, or the defense forces.[14]

Failure to Prepare Clients

Policy-makers do not control all of the elements that affect the success of their programs. Much potential for those successes lies with the clients to be served by the programs. Research in the field of education, for example, shows that client attitudes toward education—affected by the home environments of pupils—yield more influence on the success of schools than many of the policies pursued by professional educators.[15] In other fields as well, social programs depend heavily for their success on the readiness of clients to benefit from them.

While some traits of clients might be outside the control of policy-makers, it is feasible to increase the reception of program goals by appropriate cultivation of the clientele. It is possible to increase the public's awareness of a program and its requirements by attractive announcements and advertisements, designed and placed in a fashion that will attract program clients. Agencies can recruit and train personnel to counsel prospective clients about program requirements, and to improve their clients' capacity to absorb agency services.

Some problems of Project Renewal derive from an inadequate sensitivity to clients' needs. Studies about client involvement in similar American programs (e.g., Community Action) indicate that the involvement of neighborhood residents increases the efficacy of program planning and the likelihood of program acceptance by local populations.[16] In this regard, Project Renewal's problems may depend partly on the feeling of neighborhood residents that their interests have not been adequately considered by those who design the projects.

Failure to Follow Established Procedures

Even the most careful planning or the most generous allocation of resources may fail to assure program implementation if administrators do not adhere to established procedures. The Israeli army's move into Lebanon in 1978—Operation Litani—suffered because of the military's failure to honor routine procedures of equipment inventory and maintenance.[17] Elsewhere, personnel in the Bank of Israel have been lax in their insistence on routine procedures for dealing with the managers of commercial banks.[18] Often such failures to honor established procedures cause no obvious damage. As in Operation Litani, however, such lapses may haunt a program when it is expected to perform at maximum effectiveness under great stress.

GROUP III: FAILURE TO ANTICIPATE PROBLEMS OF IMPLEMENTATION

A third group of problems is failure to recognize the likelihood that program implementation will be problematical. Programs do not administer themselves. Especially for activities that are new, complex, or controversial, the failure to anticipate problems in implementation is likely to invite the occurrence of those problems. However, the nature of the deficiencies listed under Group III suggests ways in which they may be overcome. The first step in dealing with problems of implementation is to recognize their likelihood.

Lack of Follow-up

Ralph Nader taught the American public that legislating program goals does not assure their implementation.[19] All the problems of implementation cited to this point suggest the need for follow-up after a program has been formally initiated. A program may be well grounded in law, but a subsequent budget may not provide sufficient funds; administrative personnel may lack sufficient training or motivation; problems of coordination or overload may lessen effectiveness; an administrative reorganization may have only superficial effects on performance; an unanticipated flaw in legislation may provide loopholes in the authority of administrators; administrators may fail to adhere to established procedures. According to Nader, program advocates must see to the implementation of their goals in administrative agencies.

Follow-up may be most essential in the case of programs likely to arouse continued opposition. Antagonists might seek to weaken a program through an inadequate budget or at numerous points of decision in the offices charged with the program's implementation. Nader has listed for the American public a variety of programs requiring the continued close attention of their advocates, programs to preserve the environment, to assure industrial health and safety, and to protect consumers from products that are unsafe, unhealthy, ineffective, or too expensive.

At times, follow-up is needed when there are few active opponents to a program, but when those in charge are simply indifferent or fail to provide sufficient resources. This was the case with a program of the Israeli Army to bring certain recruits up to a level where they could be used effectively by the military and later make a more effective contribution to the civilian economy.[20] In other instances, the Ministry of Education failed to examine the success of its financial inducements for teachers to work in development towns, [21] and the Broadcasting Authority failed to determine if its overseas broadcasts reached their target audiences.[22]

Failure to Recognize Complexity in Program Goals or Procedures

There are virtues in simplicity. Simple program goals and procedures are more readily understood by staff and clients. To pursue too many goals and to involve too many organizations threatens to cause problems of administrative overload and failures in coordination. Problems of excessive complexity can develop piecemeal and be unrecognized until it is too late. One goal after another can be added to a program until the problems overwhelm the benefits.

One program to prevent hotel fires suffered from a structure burdened with numerous participants, overlapping responsibilities, and confused criteria.[23] Participants included the Ministry of Health, the police, local fire brigades, and municipal planning departments. Important functions integral to the program were not clearly assigned to any of the participating agencies. It was a condition ripe for each participant to deny responsibility for checking on a hotel's compliance with important regulations. There were dangers for the public and adverse economic consequences. The complexity in regulatory responsibilities caused confusion and delay for hotel developers and managers seeking to comply with the regulations.

Earlier chapters revealed some problems of Israeli policy-makers. This chapter shows that problems do not cease once policy is made. Other difficulties occur in the actual delivery of programs to their clients. Several of these problems reflect the special character of Israel. Others are more general, and occur in many other countries as well as in Israel. There is no evidence that policy implementation is more or less problematic in Israel. To Israel's credit, there is an active state comptroller and ombudsman, whose annual reports reveal considerable activity designed to improve program performance. Cynics say that the annual character of the reports prove that problems continue without solution. Yet a fair assessment is that policy-making and policy repair are difficult. There is much that competes for the attention of policy-makers. The state comptroller may have to repeat certain conclusions several times before they attract the concern needed to begin repair. Once policy-makers and citizens recognize that policy declarations do not assure policy implementation, they take the first step along the difficult path to improve effectiveness.

CHAPTER 8

How Israelis Cope

ISRAEL IS A SMALL AND INTIMATE SOCIETY. THE state is close, and citizens' frequent contacts with it may be abrasive to them. Many citizens also participate in the state, as its policy-makers, employees, and/or soldiers. For them, the state may cause both inconvenience and qualms as to their roles in the collective.

THE ISRAELI BUREAUCRACY

There are many petty annoyances. Bureaucracy is high on the list of Israelis' laments. One of the first words of Hebrew that a newcomer learns is *pakid*, which means "clerk." Soon thereafter, the newcomer may encounter a wit who refers to the country as *Pakidstan*. Newcomers as well as natives face an ever present threat of annoyance escalating to boiling rage from the quantity and quality of encounters with government clerks. The problems are no less severe in private organizations like banks, insurance companies, and shops. A fair amount of the nation's gripes and humor is directed at the bureaucracy. Further, bureaucrats are usually one of the reasons given by people when explaining why they chose to emigrate. While these problems invite some levity, they are also important determinants of the quality of Israeli life. I do not mean to imply that Israel has a monopoly on insensitive or irresponsible bureaucrats. Rather, people tend to view bureaucrats like taxes—theirs are the most oppressive in the world.

Several aspects of Israel's life provide the fertile ground in which bureaucracy can take root and serve to lower the quality of their relations with one another and their citizen-clients. The prominence of large, noncompetitive organizations in the economy is one such aspect. Not only are there ministries and other government offices, but government-owned corporations dominate several sectors of the economy. Other large organizations like the Histadrut and Jewish Agency are technically nongovernmental, but enjoy monopolistic or near monopolistic control over their sectors, including virtual powers of taxation over clients.

Compounding the problem of large, noncompetitive organizations is the propensity to coordinate or control them by a small number of key actors. Despite Jews' international reputation for great personal wealth, Israel lacks sufficient private resources. As in other developing countries, growth depends heavily on public funds. The demands of ministries and government-owned corporations pass through the budget department of the Finance Ministry and the cabinet's economic committee. Financial plans of nongovernmental bodies follow a similar path as they seek government guarantees for their loans, operating subsidies, or partial government ownership of new ventures.

Even where the formal rules do not force central coordination, the tightly knit character of Israel's elites encourages it. Key personnel in different departments of the government, the Histadrut, and the Jewish Agency tend to know one another. They move in their careers among positions in the military, a ministry, corporations of the government, units of the Jewish Agency, and, the Histadrut. Such mobility increases contacts and awareness of what is happening in other offices. Some officials serve in several organizations simultaneously. A deputy city manager of Jerusalem once served concurrently as a ranking officer of El Al airlines. It is customary for bureaucrats in the Finance Ministry or other ministries to serve on the boards of firms owned by the government. It is not easy to keep a secret in these webs of official and unofficial relationships.

It is difficult for individuals to deal with large organizations that lack a competitive drive to do well by their clients or employees. It may be even more difficult when the organizations develop and live according to no uniform patterns. One observer has found four strands of bureaucratic culture mixed together in Israel[1]:

- a traditional Middle Eastern style, which combines slowness in transacting business, deference to authority, displays of officiousness, and an inclination toward bargaining the details of official decisions.
- a British legacy that appears in certain laws and procedures left over from the Mandate period (1919–48), along with British predispositions to no-nonsense central control, leaving little room for bargaining.
- diverse traditions brought by Jewish settlers from their countries of origin, which mixes different cultures in the same workplace, thereby making it a likely breeding ground for misunderstandings and conflict.
- a self-styled Israeli approach identified with Zionist pioneers who were skilled in political infighting, confident in their inherent visionary powers and commit-

ted to pragmatism, adaptability, and improvisation that verges on lack of respect for rational planning.

Along with this variety of administrative cultures is a confusing melange of bureaucratic forms. Organizations have grown willy-nilly, with all the jumbled appearance of Middle Eastern cities whose lack of physical order frustrates efficient transportation. Like the traveler who must find directions through the streets of ancient Jerusalem, Acre, or Jaffa, the client or employee of Israel's bureaucracy is bound to encounter a convoluted route with unexpected turns and dead ends.

A map of Israel's public corporations illustrates the problem; their structure is difficult to comprehend. Some corporations are wholly owned by the government and by other public bodies, like the Histadrut, the Jewish Agency, and the municipalities. There are also joint ventures among corporations owned by these bodies and with private investors. Public corporations spin off subsidiaries; their subsidiaries produce further subsidiaries; and the subsidiaries of subsidiaries have their own subsidiaries. Estimates of the number of government corporations range from the hundreds to the thousands, depending on the definitions employed. Responsibility is most blurred in the case of joint ventures and subsidiaries. Some structures are made obscure deliberately so they can do business with firms that will not admit an Israeli connection. Units that enjoy the benefits of public support escape government controls as they deal with clients and employees. There is a perverse mixture of big government, imperfectly coordinated, that leaves individual activities uncontrolled either by free market competition or effective bureaucracy.[2]

One product of complex cultures and structures is the disparity between official pronouncements and actual behavior. There is a surplus of rules and regulations, only some of which are enforced. Rules are promulgated by proponents of certain policies or bureaucratic traditions who

are naive about related issues that tend to frustrate implementation. Important aspects of tax reforms enacted in
1975 and 1976 met with widespread noncompliance. Some
details, like requirements for certain businesses to keep records or collect taxes from their customers, were all but
abandoned by administrators who came to realize that they
were impossible to enforce.[3]

These and similar experiences leave clients and members of an organization guessing as to which rules are serious and which will not be enforced. At times there is an escalating spiral: noncompliance induces bureaucrats to
devise more rules and control procedures, which induce
clients and officers to calculate probabilities of enforcement
and risk noncompliance, which produces the partial enforcement of existing rules and the addition of new rules in
a fancied effort to limit noncompliance.

ISRAEL'S OMBUDSMEN

Like other countries, Israel has created ombudsmen to help
citizens cope. The ombudsmen will help individuals to receive services actually due to them or to avoid unjust appli-
cations of government controls. The typical ombudsman is
empowered to receive complaints, present them for comment to the office that is the target of the complaint, and—if
the ombudsman judges the complaint to be valid—to bring
the pressure of its office upon errant bureaucrats. Not sur-
prisingly, the complexity of the Israeli government im-
pinges on this complaint system. Israelis face a national
ombudsman located in the office of the state comptroller,
plus specialized ombudsmen in certain ministries and municipalities; there are no clear lines of division between
them. The national ombudsman deals with numerous issues technically in the jurisdiction of ministerial and municipal ombudsmen. Where to turn is a question that needs to

be asked whenever contact with an ombudsman is in order. Moreover, the ombudsman's own staff has problems. The national ombudsman's *1976 Annual Report* mentioned local offices that failed to enforce proper decisions despite court orders and repeated contacts. (Perhaps the national ombudsman should have contacted a municipal ombudsman.)

The System Is Too Well-Established: Everyone for Themselves!

Israel conveys the impression of being a new country with exciting opportunities for individual initiative. From the perspective of members and clients, however, its bureaucracies appear hidebound and entrenched. While the state is new, the nation is old. Moreover, the state did not appear as a blank slate; it developed from roots going far back in Ottoman and British, as well as Jewish, history.

It may be possible to reform the system in its entirety or in major dimensions. Reorganization is a venerable concept proposed by professors and consultants who deal with administration; it is also dramatic to prescribe a grand reduction of bureaucracy. Bureaucrats will face an uncertain future, as will the clients who have learned to live with each ministry's services and regulations. A better solution would be to proceed cautiously. Large-scale attempts at change are likely to be futile or superficial. It is best to assume stability in the system and seek relief for individual members and clients. This approach lacks wholeness or finality, but it fits well with general norms of reforming policy-making in manageably small steps, and with the Israeli habit of enacting rules and then devising individual exceptions. If the system is too big to change wholesale, it is possible for individuals to live better within it. Those wanting a slogan for dealing with the bureaucracy might consider "Look out for yourself." This is an admirable theme in Jewish culture, tempered by the countertheme of "Don't be a pig."

Numerous kinds of annoying encounters crop up time and again with Israeli bureaucrats. I will attempt to place them into categories that facilitate understanding, although the problems often overlap and sometimes defy categorization.

One category of problems is the lack of consideration for clients among those who design work areas and procedures. One agency-centered procedure is that of avoiding the difficult task of assessing a client's actual liability by making an arbitrarily high assessment and then requiring the client to establish the merits of anything lower. Tax authorities avoid a great deal of responsibility by using this tactic. Income tax inspectors assess high when in doubt, and force clients to prove a lower claim. In our first encounter with the Broadcasting Authority—which administers the taxes on television receivers—we explained that we had arrived in Israel in mid-1975. The statement that arrived some weeks later demanded payment of taxes retroactive to 1971—with interest and penalties. Our rejoinder brought an instruction to come to the authority's offices, with documents to prove arrival in 1975.

At times the self-serving agency can invent procedures that put clients in a classic double bind. For example, a government corporation that constructs apartment dwellings made a practice of refusing to calculate final prices before receiving a signed purchase contract. But clients could not assure themselves of financing without a final price for the apartment. An agency may neglect to send out demands for certain payments, and then levy fines on clients for failure to pay on time. It is formal policy that a client is expected to know deadlines. The Broadcasting Authority sent out late bills for taxes owed in 1976 with a fine already computer-printed on the statements. An Israeli may also have to deal with rules changed after the fact. A lengthy procedure begun under one set of assumptions may take a long detour when the rules change. Further up the scale of threat is the lack of institutional prohibition against ex post facto legislation; an action can be made illegal *after* it has been taken.

Another kind of offense shows a lack of ample training or discipline. A meeting with a clerk can be a harrowing experience as one contemplates a desk cluttered with paperwork left from previous visitors. Will my documents be treated with similar lack of respect? Probably. Will they eventually get into the right file? Hopefully. Poor work habits are also evident, as in the common scene of several clerks sitting and chatting, while others work feverishly, or several clerks hunched over each others' shoulders "kibbitzing" about one client's affairs, while other clients wait unattended.

One source of these problems may be a lack of discipline, but another is a lack of space. Clerks work uncomfortably close to one another, lacking privacy for themselves or their clients. Files pile up on windowsills and floors, perhaps because no one has taken the trouble to put them away or because there are no file cabinets conveniently accessible. Whatever the reason, the piles of material eat further into the limited space and add to the client's sense of dismay about inserting his own special case into the morass.

At its heart, the problem of space is a problem of resources. Israel is not a rich country. It has not reached the level of providing its offices with sufficient typewriters or typists. Many communications are handwritten, with all that this implies for poor communications and botched procedures. Salaries are lower on the international scale than the cost of living. Many clerks work at two jobs and some at three. Fatigue, and/or lack of discipline or concern for clients are inevitable results. Many offices have insufficient personnel to meet client demands. Receiving hours for the

public occur during only part of the working day and differ from day to day and from office to office. It may take one trip just to learn when the staff is willing to deal with you.

Limited resources also explain the lack of telephone circuits. The Communications Ministry is a major source of complaints to the ombudsman. Some applicants wait five years between submitting their requests for service and making a first call on their own phone. Space is scarce on the switchboards of government offices. It can take minutes to get into the system from the outside or for a working clerk to get an outside line. No Israeli concerned about the efficient use of time fails to keep a bit of light reading by the telephone to be perused while waiting for a switchboard operator to answer.

Part of the disorder is a mixing of personal and business matters. This, too, may be partly a problem of resources. With clerks, working at two jobs, it is tempting to use some work time to make personal phone calls. The warm-hearted clerk generates sparks when he or she entertains a child or grandchild amidst the profusion of colleagues, clients, and cluttered workspace. The child being bounced or fed on the knee of a clerk supposedly at work or allowed to crawl over the legs of strangers gives the offending clerk an unfair advantage. One defense of a frustrated client is to scream at the clerk. But who wants to scream at a parent or grandparent in the presence of a child? Even more, who wants to scream *about* the child?

Israel's service workers, like others in the economy, have developed elaborate techniques for pressing their interests with management. Sanctions are a constant threat. This means that employees will do certain tasks but not others. One day employees may refuse to receive citizen clients. Another day, they may refuse to answer the telephone, or to meet with committees assigned to define policy. The advantage of the sanction, as opposed to a complete strike, is that it allows employees to receive their salaries at the same time that work is disrupted and pressure mounts to award them increased benefits.

Bureaucrats as well as clients are hurt by scarce resources and the lack of disciplined performance. Colleagues lose their tempers with one another, just as clients occasionally let go at the clerks. As a consequence, a client may have to put up with the special burden of a hostile staff member looking for a scapegoat. Even the lowliest bureaucrats have great power. They can attack simply by entering a payment into a wrong account, putting a file at the bottom of a pile, or routing it to the wrong office. It may lie unnoticed for months while someone waits for an expected decision. Such errors may be reparable, in time, but their source may be untraceable. For example, an intentionally misrouted file can be blamed on interoffice mail. Civil service tenure provides the ultimate defense. Why bother with an investigation when it would be impossible to discipline the clerk who caused the problem?

Resource shortages produce a tendency to vague decisions. "It will be all right" is a stock comment to excuse a lack of clear commitment. Ambiguity appears at all levels. It marks relations between ministers and senior civil servants, as well as between clerks and citizen-clients. "It will be all right" can take the place of immediate budget allocations, catch-up salary increases, decisions about individual appointments and promotions, and clients' requests for mortgages or other benefits. Much of the time, in fact, it *will* be all right. There are incentives to honor personal commitments made without formal authority, so that the persons making them will be trusted next time. However, "it will be all right" may take the place of a negative decision, made in the hope that the claimant will not press the issue.

Another cluster of problems comes from procedures that are unnecessarily complex. Universities provide examples in their procedures to hire or promote faculty members. The dean of the candidate's faculty, a standing committee of the university senate, a subcommittee on appointments, as well as a committee of senior faculty members in the candidate's department, and, perhaps, a separate professional committee appointed especially for each candidate are all involved in this process. At least one, and perhaps two or three of these bodies will make a survey of recognized international experts regarding the candidate's qualifications. The complex nature of the process invites delay (two years or more may elapse between the initiation of procedures and a final decision) and assures real or imagined reports of improper behavior. There are opportunities for persons known to be unfavorable to a candidate to be placed on a committee or to be solicited as international experts for advice. An aspiring Israeli academic must look forward to this procedure several times in the course of a career—initially when being hired and then at each promotion through the ranks. By-products of such cluttered procedures are short-tempered instructors who, in turn, try to make others suffer equally.

Many complaints that Israelis express against bureaucrats are personal and immediate and fit no obvious categories. To the anxious client, the problem is simply a clerk who is rude or inattentive, who refuses to stop a personal telephone conversation, or who offers a negative or evasive answer without explaining the reason. Such problems may be open to repair by systematic efforts to arrange better physical settings for the staff and the clients, to hire more clerks, to automate more procedures, or to improve salaries throughout the economy so less of the population will exhaust itself at second and third jobs. Steps in all of these directions would do much to improve the quality of life in Israel and to lessen citizen antipathy toward state offices and services. Barring any impending changes of these kinds, however, the clients and staff members will need to assert their demands and sharpen their defenses against offenders.

SURVIVAL TACTICS: AVOIDANCE, DEFENSE, AND RETRIBUTION

How best can the behaviors described above be avoided? If a country substantially more civilized than Israel in these regards existed, one might leave for it at the earliest opportunity. Without this as a practical alternative—the grass is greener approach does not apply in a world of ubiquitous complex organizations—it may be possible to limit contacts with the most offensive procedures. For this it helps to be rich, healthy, and to have tenure. Wealth is probably the most important requirement, insofar as it offers the possibility of going elsewhere for service, regardless of additional cost. If short on health, for example, the possession of wealth allows an Israeli to avoid the low-cost clinics of the Histadrut's Sick Fund, with the long waiting, unresponsive clerks and extra procedures to obtain drugs and access to a specialist. A junior faculty member at a university also gains an important measure of freedom on the basis of personal wealth. Given financial security, such a person can risk infinite delays in a promotion decision or even rejection of tenure.

The combination of wealth, health, and tenure will not help one avoid all encounters with offensive clerks; there are still banks, airlines, tax offices, and public utilities. Wealth that is sufficiently great to permit the employment of one's own clerks for personal matters may reduce these contacts to a bare minimum, but thanks to government policies on wages, profits, and taxes, few Israelis have the wherewithal to employ a personal staff of ''arrangers.''

Israelis use several tactics to cope with their bureaucracies. The cardinal rule is to plan the encounter. Skillful clients learn as much as possible beforehand about the procedures and rules of an office. A telephone call offers its own risks of frustration, but is less costly than a visit across town that ends in failure. A plan will improve in quality to the extent that a client obtains a maximum of intelligence about what a clerk is likely to ask for, how the clerk is likely to behave in response to a case, and the options available to the clerk and the client. Important features of a plan are an anticipation of problems and a prepared series of responses to each problem that may occur.

Occasionally, one sees a display of temper in a government office that seems contrived to impose as much disorder in the affairs of a clerk as the clerk has already imposed upon the client. This can be worth the embarrassment that it risks. It can reach the clerk directly by threatening unendurable disquiet until one's case is treated properly. It can also set off a commotion sufficient to attract the attention of high ranking personnel in the organization.

A loss of temper has its place in relations among officials, as well as between citizens and officials. Meetings among ministers, senior civil servants, labor-management committees, and even professional staffers in universities and hospitals can be noisy. In the case of a tough issue, there is likely to be table-pounding, raised voices, and posturing by claimants with a well-developed sense of their own importance.

A tolerance for ambiguity can help in several kinds of interaction; among government ministers and at higher civil service levels, it is essential. Most commitments will be given prior to final clearances. All participants know that something can go awry, over and above the change in heart of the person making the commitment. Even a change in heart may be excused, if the reasons are credible. The unavoidable crisis can take precedence over the most pressing of national interests. At times, however, a recipient will want to assure that his or her matter *is* the unavoidable crisis and not simply the most pressing of national interests. In order to assure the priority of one's claim, it may be necessary to secure one's bargaining position into the future. It helps to be indispensible, not only when a commitment is made, but also when the commitment is to be delivered. A minister who goes to extremes in staking a claim for striking workers must be persistent at all stages of a settlement and scheduled payment. Otherwise, what is promised in a formal agreement may not actually reach the employees' bank accounts.

Unresponsive or irresponsible bureaucrats are not an Israeli invention or monopoly. Other countries with extensive social policies or economic controls also have their problems. Peculiar features of Israel's bureaucracy reflect the mixture of different histories in a new state. Development in Israel has been rapid, with little concern for smoothing out rough edges. Now that the population appears to have stabilized, it might be possible to look carefully at existing structures and attend to problems of management, training, and discipline. Until that occurs, however, clients must look after their own needs. Plan for the worst and hope for the best is an appropriate guide to the offices of the government and other large organizations. A passive approach is risky. Usually it is not necessary to shout; however, some assertiveness is likely to serve the citizen. Assertive behavior on the part of clients may also serve the country by sensitizing bureaucrats to clients' needs.

In some encounters with the state, Israelis expect to suffer, and they cope as best they can. This is typical of army service. The military occupies a special niche in the society; its record is impressive. The enemy is close, and widely viewed as threatening the society that has already suffered much throughout history. Virtually all adults serve in the military and many males have experienced combat. A great number have lost relatives or close friends. Thus, public criticism of the army is not taken lightly, though there may be much griping about it among friends.

Physical deprivation is one feature of army service.

Accommodations are simple at best; cold is likely to be a problem in winter, and heat in summer; there is little privacy; and dignity suffers under discipline. The work can be strenuous to the point of pain. Even in peacetime, there is an element of danger in training and patrol.

Conscience is another problem of military service. Inner conflict may have reached its height during 1982 and 1983, when Israel initiated its deep penetration of Lebanon. Introspection was not new for many of the troops who served there. Earlier they had wondered about their roles in patroling the West Bank and Gaza. It is unpleasant to govern hostile civilians, or to patrol alongside soldiers who are insensitive to the delicate issues related to a mission. Yet an army is not an organization for discussion and decision by all its participants. Just how the politically troubled Israeli soldiers deal with their self-doubts and their duty is a story with many personal variations.

CHAPTER 9

Warfare and
Welfare State

ISRAEL IS BOTH ATHENIAN AND SPARTAN. SOME
of the soldiers who went north to fight in the summer of
1982 were also activists in the peace movement. They alter-
nated between periods of combat and—while on home
leave—periods of demonstration against government policy. A few refused to serve in Lebanon. They met with the
procedures of military justice and spent some time in
prison. However, the vast majority of opponents to the war
coped with cross pressures by fighting and protesting.

THE PRIORITY OF SECURITY

While the focus of this book is domestic policy-making, we
cannot ignore the security issues that pervade Israel. Defense is the primary consumer of financial and human re-

159

sources. It preoccupies the upper reaches of government and may lessen the quality of attention that is devoted to domestic policy-making. Among the reasons for chronic trade deficits and high inflation are the demands made on the small economy by the large defense forces. Yet another reason is the softness of political leaders to domestic claimants: there is an inclination to compensate a population made weary by military pressures, partly in the hope that a high standard of living will deter emigration.

FOREIGN INFLUENCES

Much of what occurs in Israel is a response to what happens outside the borders. Since its founding in 1948, Israel has felt the effects of major economic-political events that have taken place throughout the Western democracies. These events have shaped the markets that influence Israel's economy and have provided models for Israeli policy-makers, who want to emulate what is modern and fashionable in the West.

Economic growth and vitality generally marked the period of the 1950s and 1960s throughout Western Europe, North America, Japan, Australia, New Zealand, and Israel. Some of this is traceable to the destruction wrought by World War II. Money was available to rebuild shattered economies, and a mass of human capital awaited a new infrastructure. Once the reconstruction got underway, there were annual increases in national product and personal incomes for much of the period from 1950 to 1970. Prices tended to be stable, so there was growth in real terms. Standards of living increased. At the same time, governments expanded their efforts in social welfare activities. Insurance programs for old-age pensions, sickness and accident, and unemployment improved in terms of the numbers of people covered and the generosity of the programs. Spending increased for public education, to construct hospitals and clinics, and to modernize their equipment.

Economic expansions provided the resources for these program developments. Also at work were increased demands by political parties and labor unions, plus government departments bent on expanding their programs and budgets. Economic growth rendered painless the increased budgetary allocations. There was enough for all. To be sure, there was bargaining about the shares to be allotted to each service and about the particulars of program improvements. However, pitched battles between highly antagonistic factions were generally absent. The idea of the welfare state was generally accepted. It offered something for all major segments of the population. Representatives of the working class tended to favor growth in social insurance, while those of the middle and upper classes sought improvements in secondary and higher education. Taxes increased to pay for all of this, but economic growth was great enough so that people's income after taxes—takehome pay—also increased.[1] Growth in North America and Europe meant stronger markets for Israel, while new programs meant models for emulation.

The wonderful combination of economic growth and program development stalled by the mid-1970s. Annual growth rates of national economies slowed and even declined in certain cases. Throughout Europe, foreign workers were sent home, additional applicants were denied entry, and native workers lost their jobs at greater rates than at any time since the depression of the 1930s. Jumps in the price of energy—especially in 1973 and 1974 (the Arab oil embargo) and 1979 (the collapse of the Shah of Iran)—put even greater pressure on Western economies.

The availability or shortage of economic resources may influence policy-makers. However, the economic influences are not too strong as to put policy-makers in a straitjacket without options. If economics is the dismal science, politics is the happy science.[2] Politicians may do what they can to satisfy voters, including spending money beyond the limits and realities of economic resources. While the *rate* of program expansion may have declined in the 1970s, social programs continued to expand faster than the economic growth rate. Sweden's government expenditure grew more than its national product in twenty-one of twenty-five recent years; Italy's in twenty of twenty-five years; the United States' and France's in eighteen out of twenty-five years; Germany's in sixteen out of twenty-five years; and Britain's in fifteen out of twenty-five years.[3] Part of this growth in social programming was the work of contemporary politicians, who kept upping the coverage and quality of welfare, health, and education programs. Part of the growth, however, was the work of medical advances and demographics, which boosted the number of senior citizens who lived long enough to collect their pensions. When publicly financed pensions were introduced years ago, the age of retirement was generally older than the average age at death. Now the average worker can look forward to several years of pension payments.[4]

How can policy-makers depart from a level of programming that is commensurate with economic growth? Easy. The government can spend more than current taxes will produce and increase taxes to cover the deficit. If that is unpalatable, the government can borrow for current outlays and leave its debts to future governments. Inflation is another answer. The government can authorize itself and private banks to lend more than is customary in relation to hard reserves (in other words, ''print money''). With inflation, the government can at least preserve the image of increasing government expenditures and personal incomes. Inflation also helps pay the debts leftover from previous governments. Debts will vanish in a puff of currency if inflation is high enough and if debt repayment is not linked to a cost-of-living index.

If political rivals oppose program growth, the government can seek support by creating the image of a healthy economy. It can start with optimistic predictions! During the 1960 to 1976 period, U.S. presidential advisors *overestimated* economic growth in twelve out of sixteen years and *underestimated* the growth of government spending in fourteen out of sixteen years. The German government overestimated the rate of economic growth in five out of seven recent years.[5] A government can also shift programs "off budget" so that costs no longer show up as policy issues. Program growth can continue, while the government budget actually shrinks. Existing programs can be shifted to special trust funds. Government departments that provide services can become special authorities or government companies, with separate fund-raising and accounting.[6]

Observers differ as to the current status of the welfare state. One group sees impending disaster. They write about overloaded government, welfare backlash, tax revolt, and political bankruptcy. In these views, governments offer more in services than they can support in the long run and risk popular frustration because program costs—and taxes—grow faster than take-home pay. In fact, cumulative government spending has grown five times faster than take-home pay in Sweden during a recent twenty-five year period; four and one-half times faster in Italy; two and one-half to three times faster in the United States, Britain, and France; and twice as fast in Germany.[7]

Richard Rose and Guy Peters write that Western governments are on the verge of political bankruptcy; one of the symptoms is the voters' sense that government promises more than it delivers. Confidence in government declines as does compliance with its regulations. Rose and Peters assert that there have been declines in voluntary reports of income and tax payments.[8] Voters in Denmark have given strong support to a tax-cutting advocate, and those in a number of U.S. states and localities have followed the lead of California's Proposition 13, which limited the tax revenues that could be collected.

A British polemicist, Brian Crozier, has gone beyond Rose and Peters in his diagnosis of ill-health in the body politic. Crozier blames excessive government commitments on the twin evils of universal suffrage and political parties. He would do away with both and mandate a rollback of the welfare state.[9]

Competitive parties do bid up the costs of programs. There is a tendency—labeled the ''political business cycle''—for parties in control of governments to offer increased program benefits and/or reduced taxes before elections.[10] However, the picture is not entirely one of irresponsibility. The other side of the political business cycle is that unpopular things—like tax increases or program restrictions—tend to occur after elections, when there is a long time before the next vote.

Hugh Heclo typifies observers who see a resilience built into democratic politics. To him, voters' tax revolts are part of the corrective mechanisms and not a sign of political-economic illness. Heclo asserts that it is more stylish than profound to write about overloaded governments and political bankruptcy. The fears have been expressed before from those opposed to program growth. Even boom periods have featured writers of doom.[11] In the 1970s and early 1980s, when growth indeed stalled, there were indications that voters and politicians reacted to the events in a reasonable fashion. Public opinion surveys showed a toning down of expectations. Candidates won public office after urging caution with respect to further program growth (e.g., Jimmy Carter) or actual reversals in taxation and program generosity (e.g., Ronald Reagan).

Israel saw periods of growth and stagnation along with the other Western democracies. Yet, Israel's present economic problems are more severe than those of its fellow democracies. Its per capita foreign debt and its inflation are the highest of any Western nation, and it continues to face defense pressures unrivaled elsewhere.

THE SIGNIFICANCE AND PROSPECTS OF PEACE

The principal economic distinction of Israel—and the most likely inhibitor of healthy growth—is its crushing defense burden. There has been a persistent drain on the GNP that has deprived civilian projects of resource opportunities, and there have been frequent wars to eat into the economic progress that has been achieved. Israel is the only Western country other than the United States to have experienced significant military activity after 1960. Measured by military deaths in relation to population, Israel's wars of 1967, 1973, and 1982–83 were some five times more costly than the United States' war in Vietnam.

The burdens of war on the Israeli economy raise the prospect of peace as a major issue of domestic policy-making. For the government the question is, Can it improve the domestic situation by making peace?

Some observers of Israeli politics—both within the country and abroad—feel that the Likud government, in power since 1977, has been a major obstacle to peace. Its settlement policy—relocating Jews in the territories occupied as a result of the 1967 war—is said to be a major impediment to an agreement with Arab neighbors. Those who disagree however, cite the actual record of Menachem Begin. When faced with an Arab leader willing to pursue a peace initiative (i.e., Anwar Sadat), Begin altered his stated opposition to withdrawing existing Jewish settlements and conceded to Egypt all that it demanded for itself in the Camp David negotiations. To date, Israel's willingness to make concessions with respect to the Golan Heights, the West Bank, and Gaza have not been tested by an Arab leader willing to make a peace initiative in the Sadat mode. If the Camp David process has stalled, it has done so as much because Jordanian and Palestinian participants have not been forthcoming as because the Israeli government has staked a firm position.

Should Israel take a unilateral step and cease or reverse its settlements in order to encourage other Arabs to participate in peace talks? There seems little in history or in the recent public statements of Palestinian, Jordanian, or other Arab leaders to encourage Israel in this direction. At several crucial points in the past, spokesmen for the Palestinian cause have been maximalists. They refused to accept the United Nations partition of Palestine in 1947, and they refused to make peace with the Israel that emerged after the war of 1948. Despite general comments by some Arab leaders that they will accept Israel in its 1967 borders, the recognizable Palestinian leadership has not formally given up its goals of destroying Israel.

Should Israel hold up further settlements indefinitely until the Arabs put their affairs in order and prepare themselves to make a reasonable offer? It was the earlier Israeli governments of Golda Meir and Yitzhak Rabin that established the broad outline of policy for the occupied territory. They absorbed East Jerusalem and placed military positions and settlements along the defense lines of the Jordan River, the ridge that is midway between the Jordan River and Israel's 1967 border, the Golan Heights, and Gaza. The Likud government that came to power in 1977 continued and expanded this policy by building more and larger settlements throughout the West Bank. At the same time, however, Begin's government dismantled settlements in the Sinai in order to make peace with Egypt. Without a comparable opportunity in other occupied territories, there can be no conclusion about the willingness of Begin or other Israeli prime ministers to make peace. The Arabs refused to accept Israel in its 1967 borders prior to the 1967 war. It was Arab belligerence that provoked the war of 1967 and led the way to Israel's expansion. Few Israelis have seen reason to freeze the status of the occupied territories until Arab leaders become reasonable. If the current Israeli settlements are an impediment to peace, then it appears that Arab leadership must assume a major portion of the responsibility.

What will happen if peace does come to prevail around all of Israel's borders? The several years since the peace treaty with Egypt provide some clues:

- Peace by itself will not remove the fear of war among the peacemakers. The peace with Egypt has held, but has not produced friendship or a relaxation of tensions between the countries. The Israeli-Egyptian peace is like the peace that has existed between the United States and Russia since World War II. Diplomatic relations are "correct." Tension reigns amidst suspicion and a recognition of different perspectives and alliances. In Israeli eyes, there must continue to be a strong military deterrent against the prospect of Egyptian adventurism. The Israeli Army, and not the peace treaty, continues to provide whatever sense of security the country feels about its western border.

- Peace is expensive. As in the case of the peace with Egypt, a peace with other Arab neighbors is likely to require extensive and costly redeployment of military and civilian installations. Call-ups for reserve duty will be extensive, as the army trains its personnel for the new concepts of defense that match the new strategic reality.

- Peace is likely to be partial. Even assuming the best, i.e., a signed peace with Jordan, Syria, and representatives of the Palestinians, it seems unlikely that all Arab leaders will agree. There may remain rejectionist states and Palestinians willing to serve as terrorists. The Jewish-Arab conflict in the Middle East runs deep in both cultures. Perhaps the model of Northern Ireland or Lebanon provide a clue to the future—periodic explosions of sectarian strife that are easier to ignite than to pacify.

All of the above suggest that peace may loosen some of the resources that Israel currently allocates to its defense but that their availability will not be total or sudden. Even with peace, Israeli policy-makers seem destined to cope with major defense commitments along with the demands of a sizable civilian sector. In the foreseeable future, the country will remain like Sparta as well as Athens.

NOTES

PREFACE

1. Ira Sharkansky, *The Routines of Politics* (New York: Van Nostrand, 1970).

CHAPTER 1

1. Likud is actually an alliance of parties, with its principal component parties being Herut and Liberals.
2. Reuben Lamdany, *Emigration from Israel* (Jerusalem: Falk Institute, 1982).
3. Central Bureau of Statistics, *Statistical Abstract of Israel, 1982* (Jerusalem 1982), pp. 298–309.
4. Lamdany, *Emigration*.

CHAPTER   2

1. United Nations, *Statistical Yearbook, 1979/1980* (New York: 1981).

2. Ibid. Omitting countries from the analyses that suffered greatly from World War II softened somewhat the picture of Israel's drop over the 1960-1978 period—from 72 percent of the Western average in 1960 to 51 percent in 1978.

3. Eitan Berglas, *Defense and the Economy: The Israeli-Experience* (Jerusalem: Falk Institute, 1983).

4. Ibid., p.24.

5. Nadav Halevi, *The Structure and Development of Israel's Balance of Payments* (Jerusalem: Falk Institute, 1983).

6. Jacob Metzer, *The Slowdown of Economic Growth in Israel: A Passing Phase or the End of the Big Spurt?* (Jerusalem: Falk Institute, 1983).

7. Halevi, *Structure, p. 77.*

8. Berglas, *Defense;* and Metzer, *Slowdown.*

9. Richard Rose and Guy Peters, *Can Government Go Bankrupt?* (New York: Basic Books, 1978).

10. Halevi, *Structure, p. 41.*

11. Ibid., p. 48.

12. The remainder are Israeli-born of at least the third generation.

13. Ira Sharkansky, *Wither the State? Politics and Public Enterprise in Three Countries* (Chatham, N.J.: Chatham House, 1979), ch. 3.

CHAPTER   3

1. Alex Radian and Ira Sharkansky, "The Likud Government and Domestic Policy Change," *Jerusalem Quarterly,* 18 (Winter 1981), pp. 86–100; Alex Radian and Ira Sharkansky, "Changing Domestic Policy 1977–81," in Robert O. Freed-

man, ed., *Israel in the Begin Era* (New York: Praeger, 1982), pp. 56–75.

2. *Knesset Speeches*, Aug. 3, 1977 (Hebrew).
3. Ibid., Jan 9, 1978 (Hebrew).
4. Radian and Sharkansky, "Likud Government," pp. 56–75.
5. National Consultants Ltd., "Weekly Outlook to the Stock Exchange," Bank Leumi, Tel Aviv, Feb. 3, 1983 (Hebrew).
6. *Ha'Aretz*, Feb. 2, 1982 (Hebrew).
7. Yoram Ben Porath, *The Revolution That Was Not: Ideology and Economic Policy 1977-1981* (Jerusalem: Falk Institute, 1982) (Hebrew).
8. *Knesset Speeches*, Jan. 9, 1978 (Hebrew).
9. See, for example, Aaron Wildavsky, *Politics of the Budgetary Process* (Boston: Little Brown, 1964); Ira Sharkansky, *The Routines of Politics*, (New York: Van Nostrand, 1970): Murray Edelman, *The Symbolic Uses of Politics* (Urbana: University of Illinois Press, 1964); and E. E. Schattschneider, *The Semi-Sovereign People* (New York: Holt, 1960).
10. *Al Hamishmar*, July 18, 1977 (Hebrew).
11. *Al Hamishmar*, Jan. 11, 1978 (Hebrew).
12. *Knesset Speeches*, Nov. 6, 1977 (Hebrew).
13. *Al Hamishmar*, Nov. 20, 1979 (Hebrew).
14. Knesset Speeches, July 31, 1977 (Hebrew).
15. Budget Proposal, Fiscal Year 1981, *Subsidies of Basic Commodities and Agricultural Produce*, Jerusalem, Finance Ministry, Feb. 1981 (Hebrew).
16. Ibid.
17. *Ha'aretz*, Feb. 24, 1982 (Hebrew).
18. Ibid., Dec. 28, 1981 (Hebrew).
19. Ma'ariv, Jan. 24, 1982 (Hebrew).
20. Ibid., Feb. 12, 1982 (Hebrew).
21. Ibid.
22. Micha Michaeli, "Inflation and Money in Israel after the Reform of 1977" (Jerusalem: Falk Institute, 1981) (Hebrew).
23. *Davar*, Jan. 9, 1978 (Hebrew).
24. *Knesset Speeches*, Mar. 5, 1979 (Hebrew).

25. *Ma'ariv*, Nov. 9, 1982 (Hebrew).

26. Ibid.

27. *Ma'ariv*, Aug. 2, 1982 (Hebrew).

28. *Knesset Speeches*, Nov. 11, 1980 (Hebrew).

29. *Ha'aretz*, Oct. 23, 1980, and Jan. 5, 1981 (Hebrew).

30. *Ma'ariv*, Jan. 22, 1982 (Hebrew).

31. *Ha'aretz* Mar. 26, 1982, and May 21, 1982 (Hebrew).

32. *Ha'aretz*, Apr. 1, 1982 (Hebrew).

33. See the comments by Amnon Gafne, former director general of the Finance Ministry and former governor of the Bank of Israel, *Ma'ariv*, Nov. 9, 1982 (Hebrew).

34. Radian and Sharkansky, "Changing Domestic Policy 1977-81," pp. 56–75.

35. *Ha'aretz*, Mar. 18, 1982 (Hebrew).

36. *Ha'aretz*, Feb. 22, 1982 (Hebrew).

37. *Ha'aretz*, Mar. 2, 1982 (Hebrew).

38. The recent literature of the political business cycle adds empirical weight to the role of elections. Macroanalyses in Israel and elsewhere show a tendency for governments to pass out benefits before elections and bad medicine after them. See William Nordhaus, "The Political Business Cycle," *Review of Economic Studies* 42:2 (Apr. 1975), pp. 169–90; Bruno S. Frey, "Politico-Economic Models and Cycles," *Journal of Public Economics* 9 (1978), pp. 203–20; Yoram Ben-Porath, "The Years of Plenty and the Years of Famine—A Political Business Cycle?" *Kyklos* 28 (1975), pp. 400–403: and E. R. Tufte, *Political Control of the Economy* (Princeton, N.J.: Princeton University Press, 1980).

39. *Davar*, May 27, 1982 (Hebrew).

CHAPTER   4

1. For background, see Gary S. Schiff, *Tradition and Politics: The Religious Politics of Israel* (Detroit, Mich: Wayne State University Press, 1977): also see Eliezer Don-Yehiya, "Ori-

gins and Development of the Aguda and Mafdal Parties,'' *Jerusalem Quarterly* 20 (Summer 1981), pp. 49–64.

2. Menachem Friedman, ''Religious Zealotry in Israeli Society,'' in Solomon Poll and Ernest Krausz, eds., *On Ethnic and Religious Diversity in Israel* (Ramat Gan: Bar Ilan University Institute for the Study of Ethnic and Religious Groups, 1975), pp. 91–112.

3. *Hamodea*, Nov. 6, 1981 (Hebrew).

4. Ibid., Jan. 5, 1982.

5. Ibid., Aug. 25, 26, 1981.

6. Ibid., Sept. 22, 1981.

7. Ibid., Sept. 29, 1981.

8. Ibid., Mar. 1, 1982.

9. Menachem Friedman, ''The Changing Role of the Community Rabbinate,'' *Jerusalem Quarterly*, 25 (Fall 1982), pp. 79–99.

10. *Hamodea*, Jan. 8, 1982.

11. *Al Hamishmar*, July 10, 1978 (Hebrew); *Ha'aretz*, Oct. 6, 1981 (Hebrew).

12. See Don-Yehiya, ''Aguda and Mafdal Parties,'' for its comments on Schiff, *Politics of Israel.*

13. Friedman, ''Religious Zealotry,'' pp. 91–112. In the passage quoted he is referring to a ''group formed around the Soloveichick family from Brisk.''

14. The proposal to ban football on the Sabbath is particularly sensitive to the dominant Likud members of the government coalition. This is the principal spectator sport of its working class, Jewish constituents from Asian and African backgrounds.

15. *Ma'ariv*, July 3, 1981 (Hebrew); *Hamodea*, Jan. 21, 1982, and Jan. 27, 1982.

16. *Hamodea*, July 7, 1978.

17. Ibid., Aug. 16, 1981.

18. Ibid., May 13, 1982.

19. Ibid., Jan. 21, 1982.

20. Ibid., Dec. 11, 1981.

21. *Ha'aretz*, Sept. 23, 1982.

22. *Hamodea*, Aug. 21, 1981, and Jan. 17, 1982.

23. Ibid., Jan. 7, 1982.

24. *Ha'aretz*, Mar. 18, 1982.

25. *Dvar*, Feb. 9, 1982 (Hebrew); Ha'aretz, Feb. 24, 1982, and May 7, 1982.

26. *Hamodea*, Aug. 7, 1981; *Ma'ariv*, Oct. 16, 1981.

27. *Kol Ha'ir*, Feb. 19, 1982 (Hebrew).

28. *Ma'ariv*, Feb. 2, 1983.

29. *Al Hamishmar*, Jul. 6, 1978.

30. *Ma'ariv*, Aug. 6, 1981.

31. *Yediot Aharonot*, Jan. 6, 1983 (Hebrew).

32. *Hamodea*, Feb. 25, 1982.

33. *Ha'aretz*, Mar. 25, 1982.

34. *Yediot Aharonot*, Feb. 28, 1983.

35. *Hamodea*, Feb. 23, 1982.

36. *Ma'ariv*, Nov. 4, 1982.

37. Ibid., Jan. 8, 1982.

38. *Hamodea*, Jan. 14, 1982, and Mar. 31, 1982.

39. *Ma'ariv*, Dec. 2, 1982: *Kol Ha'ir*, Mar. 4, 1983.

40. *Hamodea*, May 7, 1982.

41. *Ma'ariv*, Nov. 11, 1982.

42. Ibid., Feb. 12, 1982.

43. *Hamodea*, Feb. 2, 1982, and Aug. 25, 1982.

44. Ibid., Jan. 19, 1982.

CHAPTER 5

1. A representative bibliography appears in Aaron Wildavsky, *Budgeting: A Comparative Theory of Budgetary Processes* (Boston, Mass.: Little, Brown, 1975).

2. Naomi Caiden and Aaron Wildavsky, *Planning and Budgeting in Poor Countries* (New York: Wiley, 1974), especially ch. 3.

3. Bank of Israel, *Annual Report, 1981*, Jerusalem, p. 40; National Consultants Ltd., "Weekly Outlook to the Stock Exchange," Tel Aviv, Bank Leumi, Feb. 3, 1983 (Hebrew).

4. State Comptroller, *Annual Report No. 32* (Jerusalem, 1982), p. 14. Note that these figures do not include much of the spending of municipal authorities or of government-owned companies.

5. The 1981 devaluation was 105 percent, while the CPI increased 117 percent. For 1982, the devaluation was 114 percent, while the CPI increased 131 percent. Throughout much of 1983, devaluations continued to lag behind inflation. In October of 1983, there was a devaluation of 23 percent that was meant to correct this lag, at least partly.

6. The Bank of Israel *Annual Report, 1981* says that government spending increased 104 and 144 percent in 1979 and 1980, while the GNP increased in the same years 98 and 140 percent. The lack of correspondence between these figures and those for government budgets as reported by the state comptroller referred to in note 4 above reflect the wider scope of Bank of Israel research, its care to measure spending that is "off budget," and its use of the calendar year instead of the Israeli fiscal year for its analysis.

7. In the year ending with the third quarter of 1981, for example, incomes increased 98 percent while the CPI increased 116 percent (see Bank of Israel *Annual Report, 1981* [Hebrew]).

8. See the comments of Arnon Gafne, former director general of the Finance Ministry and governor of the Bank of Israel, in *Ma'ariv*, Nov. 9, 1982; and *Dvar*, May 27, 1982 (Hebrew). For an economist's discussion of the causes of the recent inflation, see Micah Michaeli, *Inflation and Money in Israel after the Reform of 1977*, (Jerusalem: Falk Institute, 1981) (Hebrew).

9. Hugh Heclo and Aaron Wildavsky, *The Private Government of Public Money: Community and Policy Inside British Public Administration* (London: Macmillan, 1974); Patrick Weller and James Cutt, *Treasury Control in Australia* (Sydney, Australia: Ian Novak, 1976). The material for the description and analysis reported below comes from interviews con-

ducted by the author with personnel in the following organizations: Finance Ministry (including the Budget Department and the Accountant General's Department); Ministry
of Housing and Building; Ministry of Health; Interior Ministry; Bank of Israel; State Comptroller; El Al-Israel Airlines; and the municipalities of Tel Aviv and Jerusalem.

10. Charles E. Lindblom, "Decision-Making in Taxation and
Expenditure," in *Public Finances: Needs, Sources, Utilization*,
National Bureau of Economic Research Special Conference
Series, 12 (Princeton, N.J.: Princeton University Press,
1961).

11. Ira Sharkansky, *The Routines of Politics* (New York: Van
Nostrand, 1970).

12. In Israel the director general is the senior official in a ministry, just below the minister. Directors general are appointed and removed by the government upon the recom-
mendation of the minister. Typically, they have a
professional background relevant to the work of the ministry and thereby serve as a bridge between the political and
technocratic layers.

13. Aaron Wildavsky, *The Politics of the Budgetary Process* (Boston, Mass.: Little, Brown, 1964).

14. In January 1982, an Israeli taxpayer reached the top (60 percent) marginal bracket at an annual income equivalent to
$15,700 and at that point paid an overall rate of 37 percent of
gross income.

15. Uri La'Or, "On Budgetary Problems in a Period of Inflation," *Economic Quarterly* 100 (May, 1979), pp. 124–26.

16. See John P. Crecine, *Governmental Problem-Solving: A Com-
puter Simulation of Municipal Budgeting* (Chicago, Ill.: Rand
McNally, 1969).

17. *Ha'aretz* Oct. 23, 1980, and Jan. 5, 1981 (Hebrew).

18. A. Hecht, "Local Government in Israel and Its Problems,"
Local Finance 10 (Dec. 1981), pp. 3–14.

19. *Budgets for Local Authorities for 1982* (Jerusalem: Ministry of
the Interior), pp. 6–10 (Hebrew).

20. The emphasis on improvisation, at the expense of systematic planning, is not entirely a product of high inflation. It

has deep roots in Israeli government practice. See Benjamin Akzin and Yehezkl Dror, *National Planning in Israel* (Tel Aviv, 1966), pp. 11–12 (Hebrew).

21. Wildavsky, *Budgetary Process.*
22. Caiden and Wildavsky, *Budgeting in Poor Countries.*

CHAPTER 6

1. See, for example, Richard Rose, ed., *Challenge to Governance: Studies in Overloaded Politics* (Beverly Hills, Calif.: Sage, 1980). William A. Niskanen, Jr., *Bureaucracy and Representative Government* (Chicago, Ill.: Aldine, 1971); and Eugene Bardach, *The Implementation Game: What Happens After a Bill Becomes a Law* (Cambridge, Mass.: MIT Press, 1977).

2. See, for example, Ira Sharkansky, *Wither the State? Politics and Public Enterprise in Three Countries* (Chatham, N.J.: Chatham House, 1979), and Jeffrey Obler "Private Giving in the Welfare State, *British Journal of Political Science,* 11 (Jan. 1981), pp. 17–48.

3. D. Lindsay Keir, *The Constitutional History of Modern Britain* (London: 1943), especially pp. 383–85.

4. The foundation is not inclined to welcome outside scrutiny. Leaders of the organization expressed a concern to guard the confidentiality of their donors, to protect the schedules of senior staff, and to protect the foundation against possible embarrassment. Foundation policy is to refuse inquiries from journalists. The foundation has also resisted a probe from the Israeli state comptroller. Despite that official's sweeping power to inquire into organizations with government connections, he did not gain access to the Jerusalem Foundation. At first, the manager of the foundation sought to discourage my research or to restrict my attention to a general survey and to annual reports and other documents of the foundation. After some persuasion, she agreed to be interviewed and to authorize senior associates to answer certain specific questions in their fields of competence. I

was not welcomed to speak independently with other staff
members.

5. The Jerusalem Foundation, "Rules of the Organization,"
   mimeo (Hebrew).

6. The data come from *Annual Report, 1980,* and Jerusalem
   Municipality, "Operating Budget Proposals and Explanations, Fiscal Year 1980" (Jerusalem, 1980) (Hebrew); 1980 is
   the most recent year for which full-year data are available.

7. For example: *Kol Ha'ir* (All the City), Dec. 17, 1982 (Hebrew).

8. The possible exception is the Sapir Fund, established by the
   late Government Minister Pinhas Sapir. However, the Sapir Fund was never institutionalized to the extent of the Jerusalem Foundation.

9. In the classic formulation of George Washington Plunkitt,
   "honest graft" occurs when "I seen my opportunities and I
   took 'em." "Dishonest graft—black-mailin' gamblers, sa-
   loonkeepers, disorderly people, etc." See William L. Rior-
   don, *Plunkitt of Tammany Hall* (New York: E. P. Dutton,
   1963), pp. 3–6.

10. For example, *Kol Ha'ir,* Dec. 18, 1981 (Hebrew).

CHAPTER   7

1. See, for example, Jeffrey L. Pressman and Aaron
   Wildavsky, *Implementation* (Berkeley: University of Califor-
   nia Press, 1973); Eugene Bardach, *The Implementation Game:
   What Happens after a Bill becomes a Law* (Cambridge, Mass.:
   MIT Press, 1977); and Walter Williams, ed., *Studying Imple-
   mentation* (Chatham, N.J.: Chatham House, 1982).

2. Matthew Holden, Jr., "Imperialism in Bureaucracy,"
   American Political Science Review, 60 (Dec. 1966), pp.
   843–951.

3. State Comptroller, *Annual Report no. 31* (Jerusalem: State Comptroller, 1980), pp. 225–40. (Hebrew)

4. State Comptroller, *Annual Report no. 30* (Jerusalem: State Comptroller, 1979), pp. 34–39. (Hebrew)

5. Richard Rose, ed., *Challenge to Governance: Studies in Overloaded Politics* (Beverly Hills, Calif.: Sage, 1980).

6. *Annual Report no. 30*, pp. 418–28.

7. State Comptroller, *Review of Tel Aviv Municipality* (Jerusalem: State Comptroller, 1978), pp. 54–79. (Hebrew)

8 *Annual Report no. 31*, p. 69.

9. State Comptroller, *Annual Report no. 29* (Jerusalem: State Comptroller, 1978), pp. 617–21. (Hebrew)

10. *Annual Report no. 30*, pp. 429–63.

11. Ibid., pp. 429–47.

12. Martin Landau, "Redundancy, Rationality, and the Problem of Duplication and Overlap," *Public Administration Review*, 29 (July–Aug. 1969), pp. 346–58.

13. *Annual Report no. 30*, pp. 490–96.

14. *Annual Report no. 29*, pp. 486–95.

15. See James S. Coleman, et al., *Equality of Educational Opportunity* (Washington, D.C.: U.S. Government Printing Office, 1966).

16. See, for example, Richard C. Cole, *Citizen Participation and the Urban Political Process* (Lexington, Mass.: D. C. Heath, 1974), and Douglas Yates, *Neighborhood Government* (Lexington, Mass.: D. C. Heath, 1973).

17. *Annual Report no. 29*, pp. 700–710.

18. Ibid., pp. 815–36.

19. See, for example, E. F. Cox, R. C. Fellmeth, and J. E. Schulz, *Nader's Raiders* (New York: Grove, 1969), and M. J. Green, ed., *The Other Government: The Unseen Power of Washington Lawyers* (New York: Norton, 1978).

20. *Annual Report no. 29*, pp. 742–45.

21. *Annual Report no. 30*, pp. 295–99.

22. Ibid., pp. 930–32.

23. Ibid., pp. 598–600.

CHAPTER 8

1. Gerald E. Caiden, *Israel's Administrative Culture* (Berkeley: University of California, Institute of Government Studies, 1970).

2. Ira Sharkansky, *Wither the State? Politics and Public Enterprise in Three Countries* (Chatham, N.J.: Chatham House, 1979), esp. ch. 3.

3. Alex Radian and Ira Sharkansky, "Tax Reform in Israel: Partial Implementation of Ambitious Goals," *Policy Analysis*, (Summer 1979).

CHAPTER 9

1. Richard Rose and Guy Peters, *Can Government Go Bankrupt?* (New York: Basic Books, 1978); Peter Flora and Arnold J. Heidenheimer, eds., *The Development of Welfare States in Europe and America* (New Brunswick, N.J.: Transaction Books, 1981).

2. Rose and Peters, *Can Governments Go Bankrupt?*

3. Ibid., ch. 2.

4. Ibid., ch. 5.

5. Ibid., ch. 6.

6. Ira Sharkansky, *Wither the State? Politics and Public Enterprise in Three Countries* (Chatham, N.J.: Chatham House, 1979); Rose and Peters, *Can Governments Go Bankrupt?*, pp. 144–49.

7. Ibid., ch. 2.

8. Ibid., p. 209.

9. Brian Crozier, *The Minimum State: Beyond Party Politics* (London: Hamish Hamilton, 1979).

10. William Nordhaus, "The Political Business Cycle," *Review of Economic Studies* 42:2 (Apr. 1975), pp. 169–90; Duncan MacRae, "A Political Model of the Business Cycles," *Journal of Political Economy* 85 (Apr. 1977), pp. 239–63.

11. Hugh Heclo, "Toward a New Welfare State?" in Flora and Heidenheimer, *Europe and America*, pp. 383–406.

INDEX

181